T0194588

The Captain's Log

Leadership and Sailing:
Discovering the Biblical Connections

John Piotraschke

WESTBOW
PRESS®
A DIVISION OF THOMAS NELSON
& ZONDERVAN

WestBow Press books may be ordered through booksellers or by contacting:

WestBow Press
A Division of Thomas Nelson & Zondervan
1663 Liberty Drive
Bloomington, IN 47403
www.westbowpress.com
844-714-3454

Front and back cover artwork by Kelly Gau

ISBN: 978-1-6642-4478-8 (sc)
ISBN: 978-1-6642-4479-5 (hc)
ISBN: 978-1-6642-4477-1 (e)

Library of Congress Control Number: 2021918874

Print information available on the last page.

WestBow Press rev. date: 09/22/2021

It is my desire to recognize two people who have made an indelible impact on me and my life.

First, my dad. His insistence on discipline and excellence were catalysts for me as I entered the world of work. He was tough and expected a lot. As I look back, I'm glad he was.

Second is my wife, Cheryl. She is simply the greatest leader I have ever known. I've been the benefactor of her love and wisdom for almost thirty-five years. She is a remarkable human. As I write and as you read, their fingerprints are all over this work.

Contents

Foreword xi

Acknowledgments xiii

From the Cockpit xv

Considerations of Faith xvii

Leadership Principles xix

Introduction xxi

Principle #1   The Anchor Holds 1

Principle #2   The Cross before Us 9

Principle #3   Plot the Course 17

Principle #4   Know Your Crew 25

Principle #5   Know the Signs 33

Principle #6   Get in the Boat 41

Principle #7   Communicate Your Position 47

Principle #8   Prepare to Come About 53

Principle #9   Sense the Wind 63

Principle #10   The Holy Spirit and the Wind 71

Principle #11   Patience 77

Principle #12   Patience ... Round #2 85

Principle #13   The Motorboat and the Sail 93

Principle #14   The Companionway 101

Principle #15 Waiting for God 107

Principle #16 The Fragility of Sailboats 115

Principle #17 Below the Waterline 121

Principle #18 The Rudder and the Tongue 131

Principle #19 All Lines Are Organized 139

Principle #20 All Hands on Deck 145

Principle #21 Man Overboard 153

Principle #22 A Time to Be Captain 167

Epilogue 173

Appendix A 175

References 187

Foreword

Much of Jesus's ministry took place near important bodies of water—the Sea of Galilee, the Jordan River, and the Dead Sea. Sea vessels and water were critical to Jesus and to the development of his team. Jesus, on occasion, used a boat as a pulpit. He used a boat to get away for private time with his disciples. He used a boat to get them out on the open sea so they could together experience a great storm, so he could reveal his glory to them, and so they could come to see him as God wrapped in flesh. Jesus, together with Peter, walked on water as Peter climbed out of a boat, to the amazement of the rest of the team. There are so many critical life lessons that can be derived from experiencing the waters by leaving the shore and climbing into a boat.

I have known my friend John for more than two decades. He, undoubtedly, is one of my closest and dearest friends. Some of my most cherished moments and fondest memories have been experienced during our fellowship. He is closer to me than a brother. There are many things that have blessed me about his life but none more than his continual pursuit of excellence in helping and developing leaders. John possesses a gift in the arena of developing leaders and has dedicated his life to honing this gift into an art.

Every leader, at some point, comes to the place where reflection, refreshing, and refocusing are necessary. The principles John will share with you in *The Captain's Log* will help you, as a leader, do exactly that. You will experience the artistry come alive before you as you embark upon this journey with the captain. John does a brilliant job in weaving the intricacies of sailing with principles from God's word and with personal reflection. He will lead you step by step in meaningful, and hopefully life changing, discoveries while on the vessel that will stay with you long after you have returned to shore. My prayer for you is that your life will never be the same again.

Happy sailing!
George Marin

Acknowledgments

Two people have worked tirelessly editing and offering commentary on this manuscript. I am indebted to them for their persistence and passion. My daughter, Lauryn, spent hours editing and suggesting revisions; her insight and wisdom was priceless. My wife, Cheryl, patiently waded through every word on every page and made invaluable suggestions. Without their commitment, this project would remain incomplete. Throughout this process, they continued to fill my sails. I am forever grateful.

My career was blessed by many incredibly talented leaders and educators. I learned so much by serving with them. I would be remiss if I didn't acknowledge their contribution to my experience and this writing. My friends and colleagues at Hawthorne—you allowed me to begin my leadership work. You were patient, forgiving, and oh so committed. Thank you for allowing me to be a part of the Hawthorne story.

To my fellow Giraffes at Hayes: There are no words, only a very deep, heartfelt gratitude for all we shared. Once a Giraffe, always a Giraffe.

Dr. Kim Hiel served as the superintendent of the school district where I worked as the director of teaching and learning. Her insight into racial equity forever changed me. In the years that I worked with her, we formed an incredible friendship and professional relationship. She is making a dent in this universe. Being on her team was an honor.

Dr. Peggy Flathmann also served as the superintendent of the school district where I was a principal for seventeen years. Her work and character had a profound impact on my work and life. Regardless of how great the storm was, she always maintained a peaceful presence; she was always respectful and thoughtful. I am indebted to both these leaders for the impact they made on my life.

Lastly, Bill Tessman served as my mentor as I began my professional career in leadership. I was privileged to work with him for six years prior to becoming a principal. His counsel and coaching made a significant impact on me as I set sail into the world of leadership. I don't think a week has gone by in which I didn't think about him and his contribution to my life.

The names used throughout the book are fictional except for Pastor G. The situations have also been fictionalized to remove any question of identity.

From the Cockpit

I've spent most of my life in leadership. I started as the community-organizing kid down the street and in adulthood spent thirty-five years in public education as a teacher, then head of school (principal), and finally director of teaching and learning. I have developed and organized two nonprofits and facilitated workshops around the United States as a consultant for the International Baccalaureate Organization. Leadership has been my life.

My formal education consists of an undergraduate degree from the University of Minnesota—Twin Cities—and two graduate degrees from St. Cloud State University focusing on leadership. Professionally, I have attended many conferences and workshops designed to grow as a leader. Discussing leadership, studying effective leaders, considering the millions of dimensions of leadership, and working to develop leaders has been at the heart of my work.

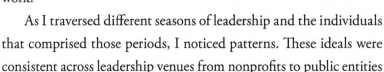

As I traversed different seasons of leadership and the individuals that comprised those periods, I noticed patterns. These ideals were consistent across leadership venues from nonprofits to public entities to small businesses to religious organizations. Two commonalities became clear:

First, all leaders do similar things. Leaders plan strategically; they communicate and have teams they must understand. They solve problems, inspire, motivate, dream, and have visions of future successes.

Second, all leaders wear out. Leaders get to a place in their existence where they feel they face a wall. Burnout, fatigue, feelings of abandonment, frustration, conflict, and lack of patience are common experiences for leaders in all walks of life.

The Captain's Log was developed with the leader in mind. Organizations cannot be healthy if the leader isn't healthy. The principles of reviving, restoring, and reviewing were not developed by accident. They are interconnected concepts that move to the heart of helping leaders grow themselves and their organizations. The principles studied as part of *The Captain's Log* are taken from literally thousands of interactions at the helm of leadership. Sometimes they are my experiences, other times friends and colleagues contributed to their development. Because sailing is a passion of mine, I worked to combine these two passions into one resource. My prayer is, as you experience *The Captain's Log,* that the wind of God would fill your soul—and your sails—and carry your life and ministry to destinations of which you've only dreamed.

God bless you.

Considerations of Faith

Before we leave the dock and link sailing with biblical principles of leadership, I feel it necessary to express my faith and seek to explain to you what I believe and who I am as a person. Sails up!

- The Bible is the inerrant, inspired word of God.
- The Bible spells out very clearly what is displeasing to God. If there are things in the Bible that are hard for you to accept, give it to God. As I meander through middle age, I still struggle with certain biblical passages. I will give the Creator of the universe credit for knowing it all, and I will remain open to the transforming power of the Holy Spirit.

- Jesus Christ is the son of God. Fully God and fully man, he was sent to earth to show humans God and redeem us from our sin. He died on the cross at Calvary and was raised three days later. He ascended into Heaven and is now seated at the right hand of the Father. "For it is by grace you have been saved, through faith—and this is not from yourselves, it is the gift of God—not by works, so that no one can boast" (Ephesians 2:8–9 NIV).

- God is loving and forgiving and wants no one to perish. He wants all human lives to be saved.
- I will not judge anyone. I will not judge any life, decision, or choice, but I will guide, coach, and speak up when people I love drift from biblical principles and do things displeasing to God.
- Much harm has been done historically by people who proclaimed Christianity.
- I am a white male and fully aware of the privilege I have living in the United States.
- Love conquers all. No matter who, what, when, where, or why, love conquers all.

Leadership Principles

Principle #1: The Anchor Holds

Principle #2: The Cross before Us

Principle #3: Plot the Course

Principle #4: Know Your Crew

Principle #5: Know the Signs

Principle #6: Get in the Boat

Principle #7: Communicate Your Position

Principle #8: Prepare to Come About

Principle #9: Sense the Wind

Principle #10: The Holy Spirit and the Wind

Principle #11: Patience

Principle #12: Patience (Round #2)

Principle #13: The Motorboat and the Sailboat

Principle #14: The Companionway

Principle #15: Waiting on God

Principle #16: The Fragility of Sailboats

Principle #17: Below the Waterline

Principle #18: The Rudder and the Tongue

Principle #19: All Lines Are Organized

Principle #20: All Hands on Deck

Principle #21: Man Overboard

Principle #22: A Time to Be the Captain

Introduction

As we sail through *The Captain's Log,* we will unpack a series of leadership principles. These principles will be taught and reflected upon using biblical references and symbolism embedded in sailing. Each principle begins with a short story or explanation connected to some aspect of sailing. Following the description, an enduring, reflective question is posed and biblical references cited. Sometimes there are specific scriptures to embellish the principle and sometimes there are topics from specific areas of the Bible. The biblical connections are followed by two additional sections: "The Nautical Chart" and "On the Water." The "Nautical Chart" is a brief inquiry or study of the leadership principles in which I expound on key variables associated with each. Summations, editorials, commentary on biblical teachings and quotes are all part of this section. "On the Water" is a collection of personal experiences and stories that are meant to make the principle come alive. "The First Mate's Log" is an opportunity for the reader to document and calibrate thoughts and experiences about the preceding principle.

Then they cried out to the Lord in their trouble, and he brought them out of their distress. He stilled the storm to a murmur, and the waves of the sea were hushed. They rejoiced when the waves grew quiet. Then He guided them to the harbor they longed for. (Psalm 107:28–30 HCSB)

Principle #1

The Anchor Holds

An anchor lowered to the seabed holds the vessel in place. When properly anchored, a sailboat can weather much—even in a fierce storm, the anchor will hold. A  robust gale, large waves—all are no match for an anchor properly placed. Its purpose is crucial as the safety of the crew and the vessel itself depends upon it holding. As believers, our anchor is Christ. It's that simple. Our anchor is secured by praying, dwelling on God's word, and surrounding ourselves with those who encourage and grow our faith. When our anchor has not been properly set, it can drag and be easily moved by the weather and life's storms.

Is your anchor holding?

We have this hope as an anchor for the soul, firm and secure. It enters the inner sanctuary behind the curtain. (Hebrews 6:19 NIV)

Confronting a storm is like fighting God. All the powers in the universe seem to be against you and, in an extraordinary way, your irrelevance is at the same time both humbling and exalting. (Francis LeGrande)

Nautical Chart

We are living in unsettling times. I'm sure each era and generation has said something to this effect, but we are faced with unsettling news every day—in our neighborhoods, cities, and towns. We find unsettling news in our nation and internationally. As followers of Jesus, it is our duty to pray, and there are so many things to pray about.

One tool I have used for decades to guide my prayer life is the ACTS acronym. It provides a structure that guides our prayers.

A—Adoration

Spend time adoring God and honoring Him for who He is. I often reference His creation, His forgiveness, His grace and mercy. It's a great opportunity to honor and worship God.

C—Confession

Confess the things displeasing to God. "If we confess our sins, he is faithful and just and will forgive our sins and purify us" (1 John 1:9 NIV).

T—Thanksgiving

Tell God what you are grateful for. Tell Him what you appreciate.

S—Supplication

Place your requests before God. Tell Him what you want and what you need.

As I applied this over the years, I found that when I do a good job of praying through the first three steps, the last one often isn't needed.

Does your soul have an anchor?

> Anchor as though you plan to stay for weeks, even
> if you intend to leave in an hour. (Tommy Moran)

On the Water

When I meet with an individual or group, I make a habit of checking in with everyone before we begin working through our agenda. I have made this a practice for years. Throughout my journey, I've utilized several different methods from structured go-arounds to simple share-outs, all designed to check in with people before we start the meeting.

In my last position, I was trained to use a tool called the Courageous Conversation Compass to understand where each person is at and how they are experiencing their work. The compass assesses an individual's state using four descriptors: thinking, acting, feeling, and believing (Glenn Singleton). Each descriptor represents a quadrant or zone of the entire compass. During our check-ins, we individually assess and share where we are on the compass.

One team member might address the group and identify as being in the "feeling zone" because they have been bombarded by a plethora of emotionally charged situations. Another might say that they are in the "acting zone." They've just concluded a strong, vibrant learning situation, and they are ready to fire up the implementation machine and make some changes. The preference is for participants to be somewhere in the middle. This means that their energy is spread evenly across the zones. When someone is in such a state, we say that they are "centered."

As a leader, it is important to remain centered. Okay, I'm sure that last sentence hit a nerve. I mean, let's be real, right? You are challenged each day on various levels. We cannot go through a day of leadership and be free from the onslaught of experiences that move us from zone to zone and back again. An angry employee will force us into the feeling zone. Team members complaining about the facility might provoke action. A serious conversation might challenge our beliefs. The many facets of leadership may make our ability to find the center—much less stay there—seemingly impossible.

I have had numerous situations and experiences as a leader. Momentarily, every situation and story bends us toward a certain zone. It's inevitable. It's unavoidable. It will happen. And so, by acknowledging this reality,

If you engage with people and processes when you are not centered, you risk not being completely present and risk being incapable of doing the thinking, acting, believing, and feeling that is necessary to succeed in the moment.

we move forward into each situation and circumstance. When I start seeing the world sideways (my vernacular for feeling tipped over or bending), I make it a practice to do everything I can to find the center before I engage with a group, individual, or circumstance. The people you lead will become attuned to your state of being.

They will be able to read you and will intuitively know if you are not centered. If you engage with people and processes when you are not centered, you risk not being completely present and being incapable of doing the thinking, acting, believing, and feeling necessary to succeed in the moment. It is also likely your constituents will notice your state, which has the potential to move them to a temporary state of preoccupation, thus restricting intellectual energy.

So, how do you center yourself? Pray. Worship. Take a moment to yourself and say, "God's got this." Then smile and make sure the room sees that peace.

First Mate's Log

Principle #2

The Cross before Us

To me, sailboats have always maintained a certain mystic. They have unique characteristics that set them apart from other vessels. Let us pause for a moment and consider one element of a sailboat—the mast. The standing rigging of the sailboat supports the mast—the tall metal pole that rises from the center of the sailboat and towers over the vessel. The basic purpose of the mast is to carry the mainsail. As the sail absorbs the wind, the mast stands tall and strong like a lighthouse on a rocky cliff.

As we look from the bottom of the mast upward, we notice the mast intersecting with the spreaders, and a cross is formed. On a sailboat, the cross is always before us. I found it amazing and crazily coincidental that the cross on the sailboat is supported by something called the stays (forestay, backstay). As we embark on this journey of rediscovering God, and as we *revive, restore*, and *review* our leadership and work, let us focus on the cross and let us stay close to Him. Jesus deserves nothing less.

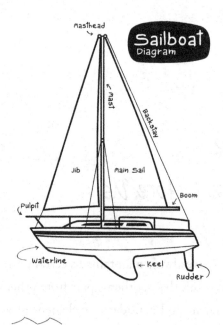

Is the cross central to your leadership?

> And whoever does not take his cross and follow me is not worthy of me. (Matthew 10:38 NIV)

> And he that doth not take his cross is not worthy of me. (Matthew 10:38 ASV)

> If you refuse to take up your cross and follow me, you are not worthy of being mine. (Matthew 10:38 NLT)

Nautical Chart

The Christian hymn "'I Have Decided to Follow Jesus" originates from India. The Indian missionary Sadhu Sundar Singh is given credit for the lyrics based on the last words of a man named Nokeng, who gave his life for the cause of Christ. Today, this song is the song of the Garo tribe of Assam, India.

As the story goes, in the mid-1800s, through the teachings of several pronounced biblical scholars, there was a spiritual revival in Wales, in which many came to a saving knowledge of Jesus. From the revival, missionaries arose, and many traveled to India to spread the gospel.

The hymn is the story of the salvation message reaching a man and his family, who were part of the Assam tribe. The Assam were an aggressive, head-hunting people and not generally accepting of outsiders. The family's conversion led many others in their village to the acceptance of the gospel message.

The chief was very displeased when he learned of the impact the gospel message was having on the tribal village. In his fury, he ordered the man and his family to come forward and renounce their faith or face immediate execution.

As the family stood before the angry chief, they remained strong and resolute in their acceptance of Christ. The tribe's chief demanded the man and his family renounce Christianity. The man stepped in front of his wife and children and stated softly, "We will not." He began to sing the song that is now a famous hymn: "I have decided to follow Jesus. I have decided to follow Jesus. I have decided to follow Jesus. No turning back, no turning back."

The chief was enraged and ordered the immediate execution of the man's children. Arrows flew from the bows of his tribe's warriors, and the children fell to the ground. As the children lay dying, the angry tribal leader arose to his feet and again demanded the man renounce his faith. "I will not," the man spoke with resolve. With tears streaming down his cheeks, he continued to sing. "Though no one joins me, still I will follow. Though no one joins me, still I will follow. Though no one joins me, still I will follow. No turning back, no turning back."

The chief was completely aghast at the man's resolve, and he ordered the immediate execution of the man's wife. Again, arrows flew. She grasped for her husband's arm as she fell slowly to the ground and died. The chief was now screaming for the man to renounce his faith. With his wife and children lying dead in the dirt next to him, he continued to sing—and as he sang, it was as though the message was being heard throughout the tribe. He sang knowing he would soon be joining his family. "The cross before me, the world behind me. The cross before me, the world behind me. The cross before me, the world behind me. No turning back, no turning back."

In the next moment, the man was struck down. As he drew his

last breath a miracle happened. The tribal leader fell to his knees and began to weep. After what seemed like hours, he finally stood tall and with tears streaming down his face, he addressed the tribe. "Today we have seen a family with strong faith. Why would a man, his wife, and children be willing to die for this Jesus that lived so long ago? This is a story of great faith. A faith that surely saves us all. Today I want to meet Jesus and be as devoted to Him as this man was. May their God become my God. May their God become *our* God."

He, along with the entire tribe, was transformed! "I belong to Jesus Christ," he announced. That day the tribal leader and the entire village accepted Christ as their Lord and Savior.

On the Water

As I wrote this book, I wondered if I should leave out faith and allow myself to consider writing about the leadership principles without using biblical guidance or references. In the end, obviously I couldn't because my faith is the artery through which all wisdom and creativity flows. For if the cross isn't before me, then I am off course. As I transitioned through the various stages of my life and work as a leader, my faith provided me with an endless portion of wisdom, insight, love, compassion, caring, ingenuity, and resourcefulness. God's provision was supernatural, beyond any explanation. My life experience is perhaps why believing is so easy for me; it's what happens in and to a life in which the cross is before all else.

First Mate's Log

Principle #3

Plot the Course

Prior to any voyage, a good captain plots the course—determining the path the ship will take, the stops made, and the ports visited. An excellent captain plans for all contingencies—weather, wind, food, time—calculating every detail. Plotting a voyage often begins with

the end in mind; the destination is defined, and the voyage's details are backward mapped. Mapping a course or plotting a voyage in leadership language is "strategic planning." Good leaders plan. They cast a vision and

plot a course to achieve the end goal. Great detail goes into this process: defining the vision and determining the steps needed to be taken today, tomorrow, next week, and next month to attain the end goal. Good captains plot a course.

Have you plotted your course?

> The plans of the diligent lead to profit as surely as haste leads to poverty. (Proverbs 21:5 NIV)

Suppose one of you wants to build a tower. Won't you first sit down and estimate the cost to see if you have enough money to complete it? For if you lay the foundation and are not able to finish it, everyone who sees it will ridicule you, saying, "This person began to build and wasn't able to finish." (Luke 14:28–30 NIV)

The planning stage of a cruise is often just as enjoyable as the voyage itself, letting one's imagination loose on all kinds of possibilities. Yet, translating dreams into reality means a lot of practical questions have to be answered. (Jimmy Cornell)

Nautical Chart

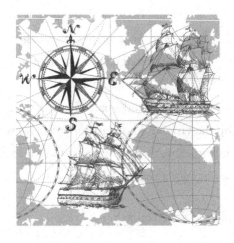

Read Genesis 3:6–19.

This passage essentially follows the sin of Adam and Eve. In it,

God states the course the serpent will follow, then speaks to Eve and the pain that will be forthcoming for women in childbirth. Finally, God addresses Adam and the labor that will be required in the future to grow food. Many scholars see God looking into the future and having victory over the forces of evil in these passages. He was unveiling a strategic plan that would last thousands of years.

Strategic planning is crucial to any leadership. Let's consider some leadership tools or ideas that can serve as a foundation for strategic planning.

> **"Without goals, and plans to reach them, you are like a ship that has set sail with no destination."**
>
> **—Fitzhugh Dodson**

1. All successful organizations have a direction. Two variables need to be defined to build unity in strategic planning. First, the leadership of the organization must define the current operational state. This is done both qualitatively and quantitatively. Surveys, data, numbers, comments, anything that speaks to the present situation is fair game. The more you know, the more you know. Second, a clear vision must be detailed. Where will we be in three years? Where will we be in five years? This picture is sculpted and arises from the work done in defining the present operational state.

2. The next step is to backward map goals and priorities. I have used the following tool many times over the years to strategically plan.

Define the present operational state	List the goals that need to be achieved next week	List the goals that will take six months to achieve	List the goals that will take 1-3 years to achieve	List the goals that will take 3-5 years to achieve	5-Year Vision Casting
In completing this, accept any data from quantitative drivers to anecdotal vignettes shared by members of the organization, including customers. Surveys, brainstorming sessions, annual reports—all are fair game and can help with this process.	This is where the action planning can really begin. Who? What? When? What must happen this week?	Continue breaking down the vision. To realize the 1-3-year goals, what must happen in the next six months?	Continue breaking down the vision. To realize the 3-5-year goals, what must happen in the next 1-3 years?	Start breaking down the long-term plan. This is where the backward mapping process begins. What must happen in the next 3-5 years for our organization to realize the vision?	Using a narrative, write a five-year vision statement. Essentially, you are writing what the present operational state will be in five years.

3. Once the present operational state is defined, the vision is cast, and goals and priorities are backward mapped, it is critical to plan for evaluating performance. This is one way to assure that all areas of the organization are moving in the same direction. Planning for and evaluating performance aligned to operational vision takes a lot of discipline. Are

your performance measures aligned to short- and long-term goals? Are there rubrics aligned to key performance indicators?

4. Action planning is the last step to consider. As you define the work that needs to be done, individuals need to be held accountable for results. Consider these questions as you begin to detail action items.

   a. Who is the task assigned to?

   b. When will it be completed?

   c. What resources are needed to complete the task?

Let your eyes look straight ahead, fix your gaze directly before you. Give careful thought to the paths of your feet and be steadfast in all your ways. Do not turn to the right or the left; keep your foot from evil. (Proverbs 4:25–27 NIV)

On the Water

Taking the helm of a new organization is hands down one of the hardest positions you will ever be in as a leader. I have found myself there a few times over the years. Each transition required me to carefully plot a course. In one instance, I found myself taking

21

over for someone who was very strong technically. He seemed to have every "t" crossed and every "i" dotted, but as I took the helm and began steering, I came face to face with problems that needed to be addressed immediately.

The biggest obstacle to my work and the vision I had for the position was that relationships were in tough shape, and trust was low. This pervaded every aspect of the department. I remember the moment when I realized the depth of the problem. Within hours of that realization, I scheduled a meeting with my supervisor, who was my biggest supporter. I explained what I was noticing. Her response is something I will never forget. She said, "I know it's bad, but that is why you are here. You have street cred. Now is a good time to use it." Hmmm. Lots to think about, right? I left that meeting, went for a walk, and pondered her advice. If I have street cred, then trust isn't the problem. It's residual negative energy left behind. The action I took was fairly simple but nonetheless critical to future success. I immediately spent time with my inner circle—the people I would work with the most. I also identified, using a sort of concentric circle design, the next layer of people with whom I needed to spend time. When I met with these teams, I did a lot of listening and asked for their opinions and ideas.

There needed to be strong ties to the different groups in the organization if the work was going to progress successfully and efficiently. I banked on my street cred and took advantage of it to initiate the change that was needed and desired. The act of listening and taking precise action changed the dynamic of the department almost overnight. Accomplishing this created the momentum and energy needed to continue the journey and take on bigger work.

What I want you to notice is that plotting a course allowed me to tackle this challenge.

Plotting the course takes on different facets depending on the work that needs to be done. There are times when you will apply the strategic planning structure that was outlined previously— perhaps even when the timeline is short. My point is, as you consider organizational improvement you must think strategically about how you will go about impacting the change that is needed. It may be as simple as meeting with those humans that are closest to you, which can be done tomorrow, or it may be a complete organizational overhaul in which you redefine the vision and structure of the entire organization.

> **"It is good to have an end to journey toward; but it is the journey that matters, in the end."**
>
> **—Ernest Hemingway**

First Mate's Log

Principle #4
Know Your Crew

Sailing longer distances often requires a crew. Leading an organization is no different. A "crew" is necessary to succeed. Leaders, like skippers, utilize the skills, talents, and abilities of their crew to accomplish the goals of the mission. A good leader knows his or her crew and regards each as a necessary cog in the wheel of the organization. It is important as leaders to know your team members—their individual talents, gifts, strengths, and weaknesses—and use that information to move the vessel.

Do you know your crew?

David's Mighty Warriors

> These are the names of David's mighty warriors: Josheb-Basshebeth, Tahkemonite, was chief of the Three; he raised his spear against eight hundred men, whom he killed in one encounter. Next to him was Eleazar son of Dodai the Ahohite. As one of the three mighty warriors, he was with David

when they taunted the Philistines gathered at Pas Dammim for battle. Then the Israelites retreated, but Eleazar stood his ground and struck down the Philistines till his hand grew tired and froze to the sword. The Lord brought about a great victory that day. The troops returned to Eleazar, but only to strip the dead. Next to him was Shammah, son of Agee the Hararite. When the Philistines banded together at a place where there was a field full of lentils, Israel's troops fled from them. But Shammah took his stand in the middle of the field. He defended it and struck the Philistines down, and the Lord brought about a great victory. (2 Samuel 23:8–12 NIV)

Nautical Chart

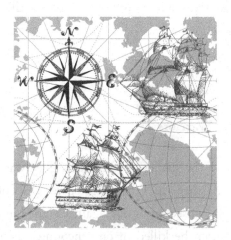

In 2 Samuel, we read about David's mighty men. Think of them as an all-star warrior team, with their skill described in considerable

detail. David knew their abilities and capitalized on their strengths. Great leaders attract greatness, don't they? The New Testament has a team that is also quite famous. Twelve men who Christ called, and together they changed the world. Two thousand years later, we are still talking about their work and impact.

I have no doubt that when David and Christ began to consider forming their teams, they sought people they believed would execute the work with precision. Consider these ideas related to building and forming teams:

1. Analyze the strengths and weaknesses of potential team members—projecting forward their contribution to the organization.
2. Use hiring structures to compare organizational priorities to the candidates being interviewed.
3. Realize talented people want to work for talented leaders.
4. A mark of a great leader is how many great people they can attract.
5. Shared values are a necessary cog in the overall functioning of any team.
6. Great leaders spend time with their teams. They get to know each member intimately: learning as much as they can about how they think, what they believe, and how they respond—honing any nuance that can be leveraged to advance the work of the organization.
7. Victories need to be celebrated and credit given where it is due.
8. Significant accomplishments need to be honored.
9. Sometimes sacrifices need to be made to sustain the work.

10. All team members must understand that they are exponentially stronger together.

> All the believers were together and had everything in common. They sold property and possessions to give to anyone who had need. Every day they continued to meet together in the temple courts. They broke bread in their homes and ate together with glad and sincere hearts, praising God and enjoying the favor of all the people. And the Lord added to their number daily those who were being saved. (Acts 2:44–47 NIV)

On the Water

The biggest, most impactful decisions you will make as a leader will exist in the realm of personnel and hiring. The decision making you do to approve hires and allow people to come aboard has the potential to positively impact every aspect of your organization. I would even suggest overall profitability and effectiveness can be defined by the decisions you make regarding personnel.

In one organization where I worked, there was a time where we had a level of synergy that was unprecedented. Every metric used to calibrate our success yielded positive outcomes. From staff surveys of organizational climate to metrics of student achievement, we excelled. After a sustained period of success, we began to talk more about our results. We really wanted to quantify what was happening and sought to answer, "What were we doing from a leadership perspective to achieve such positive results?"

One observer proposed a connection between our success and hiring practices. As we considered this connection, we began to dissect the nonnegotiables that existed within our hiring practices. We identified three

> **"There is no better tool or equipment you can have on board than a well-trained crew."**
>
> **—Larry Pardey**

practices that had become our "formula" for hiring the most talented individuals. Our data seemed to support our summations.

The process included several crucial steps. First, any candidate considered for employment had to go through three different interview levels before being offered a position. A screening interview, a committee interview—which included a representative sampling of the organization—and a team interview, where the candidate met directly with the team that he or she would be working with. All three interviews allowed us to see the candidate in a different light, and each opportunity highlighted the relative strengths and weaknesses of the potential team member.

Second, we consistently asked questions that assessed the candidate's leadership capacity. We wanted to hire leaders. When candidates showed evidence of being a leader in their personal life or in a previous professional position, we believed they would end up serving our organization in a similar manner.

Third, we were thorough when checking references. Our goal was to determine if there was indeed congruence between what we learned about the candidates during the interviews and how those perceptions connected to their previous professional life. We were exhaustive in our endeavor here. If they had previous experience with a school, I would start with the building secretary. Yes, the school secretary often offers a veritable wealth of information regarding candidates. We would also talk with the references they provided, and we would ask those individuals to speak about the candidate's qualifications for the position for which they were being considered. Notice here I did not use a canned set of questions. That type of protocol is not conducive to ascertaining the kind of information we were seeking.

Without question, this was a very successful process for inviting talent into our organization, and we saw the manifestation of this process repeated over and over. Our beliefs about this process were solidified in a couple of ways. First, these candidates came aboard and many times they immediately made a difference by engaging in the work and eventually by leading. Second, many of them left. We were quite proud of the fact that our process hired people who would move on to lead other organizations. This occurrence happened often enough for us to take notice.

As we tie this principle of knowing your crew to the dock, reflect on any dysfunction that may exist in your organization. Wonder about anything that seems off to you and then consider if maybe these symptoms can be traced back to hiring practices. I'd be willing to guess that the connection is probably stronger than what you might think.

First Mate's Log

Principle #5

Know the Signs

When planning a longer voyage over many days, a good captain does his due diligence and assesses the weather. Along the way, he wants to know what can be expected from a meteorological point of view.

Will there be ample wind? Storms? Any kind of leadership journey requires the same due diligence. Simply put, good leaders look for signs. They study the organizational patterns that can interrupt successful passage, and they react accordingly. Being surprised by some unforeseen weather-related circumstance is the very thing sailors look to avoid. Good leaders are no different. They look for signs that will steer them safely and effectively to their destination.

What are the signs?

> I will instruct you and teach you in the way you should go; I will counsel you with my loving eye on you. (Psalm 32:8 NIV)

This is what the Lord says—he who made a way through the sea, a path through the mighty waters, who drew out the chariots and horses, the army and reinforcements together, and they lay there, never to rise again extinguished, snuffed out like a wick: Forget the former things; do not dwell on the past. See, I am doing a new thing! Now it springs up; do you not perceive it? I am making a way in the wilderness and streams in the wasteland. (Isaiah 43:16–19 NIV)

What Jesus did here in Cana of Galilee was the first of the signs through which he revealed his glory; and his disciples believed in him. (John 2:11 NIV)

Nautical Chart

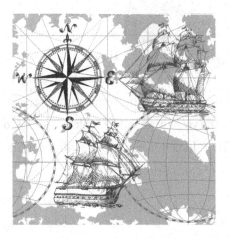

People who sail learn to read the signs of wind rather quickly. Rightly so, as this one variable impacts the ability to move the vessel more than any other. The more experienced helmsman is fairly intuitive in terms of comprehending the signs that might impact the sail. Helmsmen have learned to pick up on nuances: what is happening on shore, what the birds are doing, the feel of the air—watching a sailor with this level of intuition is really something to behold.

For the purposes of this principle, I thought it might be helpful to look at a list that refers to leadership and personal development. Experienced helmsmen share common attributes, as do experienced leaders. Here is a list of attributes that I collected from a variety of sources. Perhaps you could use the list as a sort of rubric to calibrate your own work.

Signs that you are a good leader:

1. You genuinely care about people and show empathy at critical times.
2. You are committed to seeing your team succeed.
3. You communicate effectively, and your communication is exhaustive.
4. You motivate and inspire others to be their best.
5. Those who follow you know what you expect from them.
6. You are an excellent role model and lead by emulating excellence in all situations.
7. You have the ability and humility to invest in people who can perform specific functions better than you can. You are not afraid to hire wildly talented people.
8. You excel at recognizing potential, and you are not afraid to delegate.
9. You're not afraid of giving power away.

10. You understand when to coach and when to step back.

11. You're not afraid of sticking your neck out.

12. You hold yourself accountable to results in the same way you hold your employees responsible.

13. You keep the big picture in mind, and your actions and plans reflect a strategic goal.

14. You know how to resolve conflict.

15. You see major obstacles as opportunities not problems.

16. You do not believe in failure but in learning.

17. You remain calm amid storms.

18. You are an inspiration to those around you.

19. You are predictable in your reactions to tough situations.

20. You are aware of your own emotions, ways of thinking, and body language and how they are perceived by others.

On the Water

To gauge the effectiveness of any organization, you need only assess one key variable: climate. Climate is defined by how individuals experience the work environment, and this can vary widely from person to person. The following checklist can be used to gauge climate. An effective organizational climate—one that produces positive results—might be measured by the degree with which they are focused on:

- employee contributions through innovation,
- giving employees choices and agency,
- a leadership that communicates they care about their employees,
- the leaders within the organization,
- a standard of work that continually seeks excellence,
- involving employees in decision making,
- employees feeling motivated,
- a feeling of peace and professionalism that pervades the organization.

When the organization can check these boxes regarding climate, it is likely that the organization is surfing the wave of increased productivity, quality, and innovation.

Being able to sense or read the climate of your organization is vital. Some leaders have an innate ability to intuitively read the climate of their organization; others hone this skill over time and experience. Leaders that ignore this construct fail to realize positive outcomes on any level.

The entity that achieves an organizational climate characterized by high levels of productivity, profitability, and effectiveness are places where people are valued. Their ideas, their creativity, and their passions are encouraged and appreciated, and that appreciation is expressed on a regular basis. Employees are encouraged to take risks and innovate, and they are given agency to pursue projects and passions to grow the organization. They strive to achieve excellence in their work, and there is a spirit of excellence that pervades the workplace. They are engaged in the leadership and vision of the organization. Leadership sees them as partners in the process of increasing overall effectiveness, and they are frequently brought into the decision-making process. Lastly, there is an overwhelming peace and positivity that invades every department, every meeting, and every interaction.

First Mate's Log

Principle #6

Get in the Boat

Standing on the pier is a wonderful place to behold the conditions present to any sailor. The wind is there, the motion of the waves, the subtleties of the weather that inform the voyage ahead. Merely standing on the pier allows you to capture much of what will be potentially experienced on the water. Standing, though, never results in forward movement. Standing is not sailing. To sail, you must do one thing—you must get in the boat. Pause for a moment and

ponder the leadership connections. Ideas, dreams, visions—they are nothing more than cognitive conjecture unless they are put to sea. Unless they are acted upon, they will remain merely ideas. When one stands on the pier of opportunity, casting vision and dreaming is easy. To put that dream into action and expel resources takes courage. Courage to get in the boat and get on with the voyage.

Are you standing on the pier?

Be strong and courageous, because you will lead these people to inherit the land I swore to their ancestors to give them. Be strong and very courageous. Be careful to obey all the law my servant Moses gave you; do not turn from it to the right or to the left, that you may be successful wherever you go. Keep this Book of the Law always on your lips; meditate on it day and night, so that you may be careful to do everything written in it. Then you will be prosperous and successful. Have I not commanded you? Be strong and courageous. Do not be afraid; do not be discouraged, for the Lord your God will be with you wherever you go. (Joshua 1:9 NIV)

A ship in harbor is safe, but that's not what ships are built for. (William Shedd)

You can never cross the ocean unless you have the courage to lose sight of the shore. (Christopher Columbus)

The most difficult thing is the decision to act, the rest is merely tenacity. (Amelia Earhart)

Nautical Chart

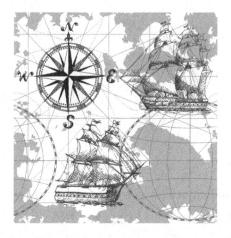

Getting into the boat is really about decision making and having the courage to move forward. It's having the courage to "get into the boat and start sailing." Decisions test a leader's character.

Tough decisions require courage—courage to act. As a leader, you will be faced with this on a regular basis. The situation Joshua faced is not drastically different than the decisions you will face. It is important to notice what happened. Where did Joshua's strength come from? His success didn't rest in human wisdom but in God.

When we are faced with risky decisions that require monetary commitment and the engagement of resources, we need to go to God in prayer. When we seek Him, we gain something beyond human understanding—we gain a heavenly perspective.

On the Water

When I find myself in conversations with leaders regarding initiatives that they are considering, we often broach the subject of getting into the boat. When I probe thinking to understand why they are delaying or not moving ahead, leaders generate the same response regardless of their type of work. When they expound on their thoughts, they simply state they are afraid—they are afraid to fail.

Risk-taking in leadership is having the courage to get in the boat. Fear will never be overcome if it is allowed to dictate thought and action. I knew a business owner years ago who was very successful. Our conversation went like this:

"Mike, what do you feel is the key to your success?"

"Not being afraid to fail. Being able to stare at the possibility of failure square in the eye and not let it control me."

"Have you ever failed?" I asked.

"Yes, I have had three businesses fail. No matter what I tried I just couldn't get the business to grow. As I look back. I would not have changed those experiences for anything. They taught me a lot about fear."

Getting in the boat becomes easier and less intimidating as we gain experience. As experience increases, so does our confidence amid challenges. We begin to think about risks differently because we have learned to calculate risks relative to failure. If you are amid contemplating an initiative, spend some time reflecting and consider the degree to which the thought of failure is controlling your thinking. Bring a couple of trusted colleagues into the conversation and together calculate your risk.

To young men contemplating a voyage,
I would say go. (Joshua Slocum)

First Mate's Log

Principle #7
Communicate Your Position

We left the slip and backed out slowly into the fairway. As we began to move forward the captain shouted, "Sound the horn!" Immediately the first mate took the aerosol horn, gave it a squeeze and the sound of the horn resonated throughout the harbor. The purpose of the blast was to make the position of the sailboat known to anyone in its path. Clear communication is critical to any level of leadership. Communicating position and purpose clarifies intent. Leadership is wrought with stories of ineptitude rooted in poor communication. The art of mastering communication begins with understanding the "five W's" (who, what, when, where, and why). Routinizing this will help maintain momentum in any organization and through any difficulty.

Is there a position that needs to be clarified?

> Moses answered the people, "Do not be afraid. Stand firm and you will see the deliverance the Lord will bring you today. The Egyptians you see today

you will never see again. The Lord will fight for you; you need only to be still." (Exodus 14:13 NIV)

"And I tell you that you are Peter, and on this rock I will build my church, and the gates of Hades will not overcome it. I will give you the keys of the kingdom of Heaven; whatever you bind on Earth will be bound in Heaven, and whatever you lose on Earth will be loosed in Heaven." Then he ordered his disciples not to tell anyone that he was the Messiah. (Matthew 16:18 NIV)

Nautical Chart

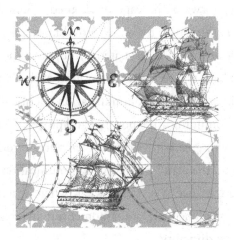

"I wish he would make a decision. He just can't make up his mind. I have no idea what I'm supposed to do. Will you talk with him? Right now, it seems everyone is moving in a different direction. Why does this have to be so complicated? I wish he would make up his mind."

These words were spoken to me many years ago following a leadership team meeting. The leader at the time had difficulty letting his position be known. Many called him a "waffler" simply because he couldn't communicate a clear position, and he seemed to change his mind each time a new voice entered the dialogue.

To understand why it is so important to clarify your position, you need only to study the dialogue above. There are consequences for not being clear.

- Employees are not happy. The emotional climate of the workplace is unsettled. The result will always be decreased efficiency.
- Attitudes become negative and, in some cases, even hostile.
- Employees are confused. They are not clear on direction and intent, and as a result their work suffers—productivity is compromised.
- Intellectual capital is being wasted. Clear, bright minds that desire to contribute to the overall organization can't and won't.

On the Water

As we set sail, consider the principle of communicating your position. You may have already agreed with the thesis that communicating your position is indeed important and that a lack of clarity has a cancerous effect on productivity and effectiveness.

There is one additional communication strategy that I used thousands of times as a leader. I call it the three-by-three rule. I'm going to illustrate my point using a request that I made of staff one spring. I needed staff to know that their end-of-year reflections were due on May 20 before we checked out for the weekend. The three-by-three rule works like this. For me to have success with the request, I had to communicate the message three times and in three different ways (a.k.a. three by three). Here's what I did:

First, I made sure I included this request as part of our weekly staff meeting. During the meeting I explained what I needed, and I asked if anyone had questions. Once we were grounded in the expectation, and I felt confident that everyone understood what to do, we moved on to the next agenda item.

During that same week, I made sure that I stopped in each department meeting to review the request and to answer any questions. Here I sought clarification.

Four days before the deadline, I sent an email reminding them of the request and that I would appreciate it if they would check in with me at a specific time to touch bases on the reflections. Essentially, I booked a department-level meeting with each team. This brought a heightened level of accountability to the request.

On Friday the twentieth, I went home with all but two reflections in hand. I had two staff members absent much of that week, and they requested a little more time, which I was happy to grant.

Not every piece of information needs to be handled this way, but it is an effective strategy to consider whenever you have information that people must know or a task that must be completed.

As we tie this principle to the dock, you should remember three important things regarding communication:

1. Identify the W's part of the communication.
2. Use the three-by-three rule whenever you have significant information or an important request to make.
3. Make a practice of overcommunicating. It's always better to have too much information than too little.

First Mate's Log

Principle #8

Prepare to Come About

"Coming about" is the process of turning the sailboat into the wind. On a tack you will change directions periodically to continue the zigzag pattern so that the sailboat can move closer to its destination. There are several things that happen almost simultaneously when the captain says, "Prepare to come about." The first mate gets ready. When the first mate is ready, the mate responds by saying, "Ready to come about." The captain then states, "Helms a lee." And they

begin turning the boat. As soon as the boat is in irons (centered in the no-sail zone) the first mate releases the jib sheet on one side and immediately cranks the winch pulling and tightening the jib sheet to the other side. While

that is happening, the captain is careful to turn slowly as the boom moves the main sail from one side of the boat to the other. Communication and coordination in this moment are critical. Clear communication and coordination are vital to any organization. The ability to create structures of communication that lead to coordination is an essential component of leadership.

> What are the structures of communication that lead
> to high levels of coordination?

First Chronicles 28:1-21 (NIV) is a relatively long passage, but I feel it captures key communication structures that are worth considering.

1. David summoned his leaders to impart vision and information.
2. He conducted a 1:1 with Solomon to discuss the vision.
3. He shared a very detailed plan with Solomon, and he had it written out.

> David summoned all the officials of Israel to assemble at Jerusalem: the officers over the tribes, the commanders of the divisions in the service of the king, the commanders of thousands and commanders of hundreds, and the officials in charge of all the property and livestock belonging to the king and his sons, together with the palace officials, the warriors and all the brave fighting men. King David rose to his feet and said: "Listen to me, my fellow Israelites, my people. I had it in my heart to build a house as a place of rest for the ark of the covenant of the Lord, for the footstool of our God, and I made plans to build it. But God said to me, 'You are not to build a house for my Name, because

you are a warrior and have shed blood.' Yet the Lord, the God of Israel, chose me from my whole family to be king over Israel forever. He chose Judah as leader, and from the tribe of Judah he chose my family, and from my father's sons he was pleased to make me king over all Israel. Of all my sons—and the Lord has given me many—he has chosen my son Solomon to sit on the throne of the kingdom of the Lord over Israel. He said to me: 'Solomon your son is the one who will build my house and my courts, for I have chosen him to be my son, and I will be his father. I will establish his kingdom forever if he is unswerving in carrying out my commands and laws, as is being done at this time.' So now I charge you in the sight of all Israel and of the assembly of the Lord, and in the hearing of our God: Be careful to follow all the commands of the Lord your God, that you may possess this good land and pass it on as an inheritance to your descendants forever. And you, my son Solomon, acknowledge the God of your father, and serve him with wholehearted devotion and with a willing mind, for the Lord searches every heart and understands every desire and every thought. If you seek him, he will be found by you; but if you forsake him, he will reject you forever. Consider now, for the Lord has chosen you to build a house as the sanctuary. Be strong and do the work." Then David gave his son Solomon the plans for the portico of the temple, its buildings, its storerooms, its upper parts, its inner rooms and the place of atonement. He gave him the plans of all that the Spirit had put in his mind for the courts of the temple of the Lord and all the surrounding rooms, for the treasuries of the temple of God and for the treasuries for the dedicated things. He gave him instructions for the divisions of the priests and Levites, and for all the work of serving in the temple of the Lord, as well as for all the articles to be used in its service. He designated the weight of gold for all the gold articles to be used in various kinds of service, and the weight of silver for all the silver articles to be used in various kinds of service: the weight of gold for the gold lampstands and their lamps, with the weight for each lampstand and its lamps; and the weight of silver for each silver lampstand and its lamps, according to the use of each lampstand; the weight of gold for each table for consecrated bread; the weight of silver for the silver tables; the weight of pure gold for the forks, sprinkling bowls and pitchers; the weight of gold for each gold dish; the weight of silver for each silver dish; and the weight of the refined gold for the altar of incense. He also gave him the plan for the chariot, that is, the cherubim of gold that spread their wings and overshadow the ark of the covenant of the Lord.

"All this," David said, "I have in writing as a result of the Lord's hand on me, and he enabled me to understand all the details of the plan." David also said to Solomon his son, "Be strong and courageous, and do the work. Do not be afraid or discouraged, for the Lord God, my God, is with you. He will not fail you or forsake you until all the work for the service of the temple of the Lord is finished. The divisions of the priests and Levites are ready for all the work on the temple of God, and every willing person skilled in any craft will help you in all the work. The officials and all the people will obey your every command." (1 Chronicles 28:1–21 NIV)

Nautical Chart

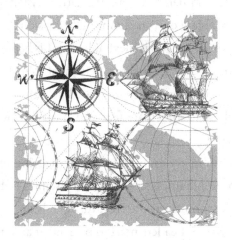

The passage I selected for this section represents several elements of effective communication: communicating vision, involving key leadership in the exposition of that vision, sharing details, delegating responsibility, and the idea of communication being coordinated (more on that later in the "On the Water" section). David is communicating a vision to the people of Israel and to Solomon—it was a word from God directing Solomon to build the temple. Let's highlight some lines of reason regarding this passage.

Lines of Reason

1. All great organizations and leaders have a vision.
2. Strong, effective leaders are good listeners.
3. The greatest vision-casting document of all time is clearly the Bible. It provides a strategic plan for our existence and the blessed life that follows. God invites us into the entire story.
4. Having a vision is one thing, but communicating that vision is quite another. Without the latter, vision will never be realized. How do you communicate vision?
5. Resistance to vision is inevitable and this happens for several reasons. Fear is the greatest detriment to realizing vision. If someone isn't having it—they are likely afraid. Good leaders learn how to anticipate fear and learn how to strategically counter it.
6. There are many examples of vision casting in the Bible— Noah, Abraham, Jesus, Paul, the disciples—the list is long.
7. Any communication regarding vision needs to be coordinated. Leaders need to be explicit about the method, modality, and timing of communication.

On the Water

I'm hoping by this point you are beginning to see some of the principles weaving together, producing a tapestry of skills and cognition that can guide your leadership.

Coordinated communication is the topic of this "On the Water" section. To illustrate this point, I'm going to borrow from a playbook that one of my supervisors used many times. She was a master when it came to coordinating communication. Whenever an important message needed to be communicated, she followed a very arduous process that guaranteed everyone in the organization would receive the information in a timely manner. She did this to stay coordinated. A decision that is far reaching—one that can touch or impact everyone in the organization—requires a detailed, coordinated communications launch.

The key members of the leadership team were all in the room when the communication structure was built. She first led us in a process of determining the groups that needed to receive the communication. They were all recorded, and we reached full consensus on this piece before moving on. Once the groups had been identified, we then defined the mode of communication that would be used. Sometimes we chose electronic means like recorded videos, formal letters, or emails. Other times we had large meetings, and occasionally we had smaller focus groups. The intent was to make sure that everyone received the same information.

The last piece to this structure was to determine timelines. This was arguably the most important step as we worked to assure everyone received the information in a timely manner. (Caution: If you leak information slowly, it erodes trust. Some employees will experience moments of privilege and others will feel like second-class citizens.) We started with a date and time detailing exactly who would receive the information and when.

When all the information was up on the white board, and we had reviewed the steps and everyone was clear, no questions, no wonderings, we would adjourn. The meetings all ended in the same way. She would look at all of us very seriously and say, "The information that we have just talked about is embargoed until the first communication goes out. Until that time nobody is to talk about this. Nobody. Clear?"

I can honestly say that nobody ever breathed a word of the information to anyone. (Now I must pause and say that I have worked in organizations where that sentiment was expressed by the leader, but by the time I got back to my department everyone knew what had taken place in the meeting. I was always baffled as to how this could be.)

If you follow this "who, how, when" process as the means of coordinating communication, you will build cohesion as an organization, and with that comes high levels of efficiency, productivity, and effectiveness. Are you feeling coordinated?

First Mate's Log

Principle #9

Sense the Wind

For a moment, allow the idea of the wind and sailing to become an image for your soul and your life interacting with God. Skilled helmsmen have a keen ability to sense and interpret the wind. They admire and perceive even subtle nuances in direction and strength. A sailor learns to sense the wind by sailing and spending time in the wind. As believers, if we are to know God, we must spend time with Him. In fact, our sense of God in our lives and at work in our lives is directly proportional to the amount of time spent with Him. By growing deeper in our love and knowledge of God, our ability to sense His presence in our lives will be magnified. Then we will ultimately discover all He has for us.

> **"We can battle the sea, or we can embrace it. Sometimes she will be sweet and sometimes mean as a snake. We must embrace the experience and trust we will get through it."**
>
> **—Michelle Segrest**

Can you sense God? Can you hear him?

He fell to the ground and heard a voice say to him, "Saul, Saul, why do you persecute me?"

"Who are you, Lord?" Saul asked. "I am Jesus, whom you are persecuting," he replied. (Acts 9:4–5 NIV)

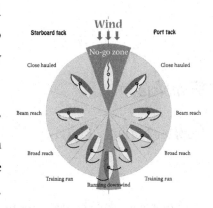

Nautical Chart

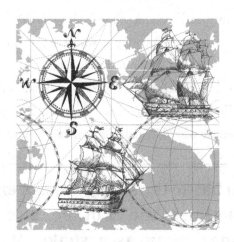

As we spend more and more time listening to God, we get to know Him better, and we are more adept at sensing His presence and hearing His voice. When I was writing this section of *The Captain's Log*, I developed a deeper appreciation for these two verses. They represent the beginning of Paul's interaction and communication with God. Let's look at his words: "Who are you, Lord?" Most commentaries suggest that he probably recognized that it was God speaking, but at this point a personal relationship with the Lord Jesus had not been established. When we consider what transpires during the rest of his life, we might conclude there is likely no human that has ever been able to sense God more clearly. His ability to sense God allowed him to write much of the New Testament. And it all started with, "Who are you, Lord?"

Lines of Consideration

1. Take a moment right now and shut everything off. If you are on the boat, excuse yourself and go find a place to be alone. Tell those aboard that it's time to work on that whole "sensing God thing." They'll understand. In your quiet time reflect on where you are regarding being able to sense God. Can you or do you need to ask as Paul did, "Who are you, Lord?"

2. I had a period that preceded a huge decision when I felt that I needed to sense God on a higher or deeper level. I read a book called *How to Listen to God*, by Charles Stanley. This book changed my life. Through reading and studying, I learned the signs God uses to speak to me. Today when I face a tough decision, I know how God will speak to me. Do you?

3. If this section has brought forth an uneasiness, pray—right now! Determine what you will do to draw nearer to the One

that is in control. What needs to change in your routine so this can happen?

The pessimist complains about the wind; the optimist expects it to change; the realist adjusts the sails. (William Arthur Ward)

On the Water

Three of the biggest stressors in life are: a major purchase, a career change/starting a new job, and formally changing the status of a relationship like getting married or divorced. During one insane period of my life, I did all three in the same week. I bought a car, started a new job, and got engaged. I wouldn't recommend it. Wait! I would recommend all three—just not in the same week. Whew! Almost missed that one.

When we are forced to make big decisions, we benefit greatly from godly wisdom. One way to define godly wisdom is a keen ability to sense what God wants us to do. How does that happen? There are several ways to approach this question, but let's start by considering the attributes of God. God is gentle, kind, peaceful, full of grace and mercy. He is abundant in love and sincerity. He listens and weighs situations fairly. When we apply ourselves to seeking God—studying his word and obeying his commands—we are slowly transformed into His image. When Bible study leads to application, we find peace. And peace is often the method that God uses to help us know if a decision is right or wrong. Have you ever found yourself saying, "I just don't have peace about that decision?" That may well be your ability to listen and sense what God is trying to tell you.

Amid big decisions, I tend to follow a pattern—meaning I do the same things with a high degree of repetition. I pray, I reflect, I get quiet, and I seek the counsel of people I am close to. When they speak, I listen intently. What I have found is that God talks to me in the middle of the night. It's quiet, it's dark, and there aren't any distractions. He has my undivided attention. It is in those moments that He delivers his verdict. If I feel peace, I sleep. If I don't feel peace, I toss and turn all night, and I know what my answer is. Listening to God is also about being obedient. I can toss and turn all night and then in the morning ignore His voice. Ignoring His voice leads to consequences that are generally, at some point, painful.

A few years ago, I accepted a new position. I was genuinely excited to move back to the school district where I got my start. It was a sunny Tuesday in May when I went to meet the staff. I spent the afternoon getting to know everyone. I left that afternoon with a very heavy heart and a sinking feeling in my gut. So many things were just not right. I spent that evening praying and reflecting and talking to my wife. I had a middle-of-the-night wrestling match with God, and He delivered a verdict: the job wasn't right for me. The next day I called and declined the position, essentially declining a position I had already accepted. This was excruciating. I had to swallow my pride and obey God's voice. God isn't always that clear, but we can be assured that He is there and will speak to us. We just must be willing to listen and follow through in obedience.

First Mate's Log

Principle #10

The Holy Spirit and the Wind

For this next principle I'd like you to think of the sails representing your life and the wind as the Holy Spirit. The wind (Holy Spirit) interacts with the sails (your life) to provide forward movement. On a sailboat, we need to be ready to receive the wind. Sails must be up—they must be free from holes—they must be trimmed properly—no luffing (sails when trimmed properly use the maximum force of the wind). Life is similar, isn't it? We need to be ready for the Holy Spirit to fill our sails. How do we do that? How do we ready our sails, so to speak? By praying, reading God's Word, obeying His commands, listening to what God is saying to us, having fellowship with other believers, memorizing scripture, and building a spiritual hunger and thirst that only God can satisfy. All these things allow the Holy Spirit more opportunity to move us forward and give our faith and ministry momentum.

So, are your sails luffing?

So, I say, walk by the Spirit, and you will not gratify the desires of the flesh. For the flesh desires what is contrary to the Spirit, and the Spirit what is contrary to the flesh. They are in conflict with each other, so that you are not to do whatever you want. But if you are led by the Spirit, you are not under the law. (Galatians 5:16–26 NIV)

I have much more to say to you, more than you can now bear. But when he, the Spirit of truth comes, he will guide you into all the truth. He will not speak on his own; he will speak only what he hears, and he will tell you what is yet to come. He will glorify me because it is from me that he will receive what he will make known to you. All that belongs to the Father is mine. That is why I said the Spirit will receive from me what he will make known to you. (John 16:12–15 NIV)

The art of the sailor is to leave nothing to chance. (Annie Van De Wiele)

Nautical Chart

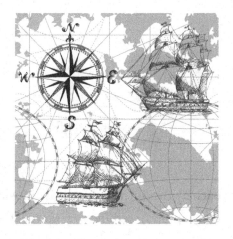

On top of the mast is a device called a windex (not the blue chemical you spray on your windows). It is a triangular-shaped mechanism with an arrow attached to it—the arrow moves according to the wind. The tip of the arrow indicates from which direction the wind is blowing. At the top of the wheel is a GPS unit that gives me my exact location. On the wheel dashboard is a panel that has a wind speed indicator and a depth indicator. These "tools" guide me. They allow for safe passage. In John 13, Jesus is talking about all that will come when the Holy Spirit enters our life—our story. In Galatians, we see the manifestation of a life lived by the Spirit. When we sail and live life, we have tools available to us that will manifest good when applied appropriately. The potential for greatness is endless when our sails—our lives—receive all that the Spirit is ready to give.

On the Water

I recently concluded an interactive exercise in which I learned a lot about the Holy Spirit. According to scripture, the Holy Spirit has two primary purposes: He guides us and works to transform our lives—guidance and transformation (happening slowly and methodically over time). With that thought in mind, consider the Holy Spirit as a guide moving in and through our lives directing and steering us in the way of God's will.

The bigger the decision, the bigger the prayer. The bigger the decision, the more time you better spend seeking godly wisdom and asking the Holy Spirit to guide you. Want to guess what the biggest deterrent to listening to the Holy Spirit is? Pride and the cancer of self-sufficiency. Unfortunately, it's a disease that permeates many souls.

I remember well one prideful moment. I was hiring a few new employees, and I had a candidate that I was excited to hire. I didn't do my due diligence and forged ahead resting on my own pride and laurels to defend the decision to hire. I sensed a couple of things during the interview process that should have raised a red flag, but because I had heard such wonderful things, I wrote it off as something in the moment. I ignored the prompts—I didn't listen,

I didn't do what I should have done—and I paid the price. Six weeks after I hired her, I fired her. She may have lit the field up in another city, but in our town, she was a dud. It was there all along, but the cancer of self-sufficiency blinded me from seeing what was apparently obvious to so many.

First Mate's Log

Principle #11

Patience

In sailing there will be times when we find ourselves in a season or period of waiting. That circumstance occurs most often for a sailor in the absence of wind. In those moments, there simply isn't anything to do but wait. Forced waiting takes patience, doesn't it? As humans we are often impatient when we don't have what we need or are forced to wait out one of life's circumstances. I think many of us would prefer to move through life under our own power and not have to rely on anyone or anything. Periods of waiting, though, are inevitable in sailing. There are marked similarities to life as a believer aren't there? Have you ever found yourself waiting on God? Waiting can be very hard. In our waiting, there seems to be a connection between the seriousness of our circumstance and the level of impatience we feel toward God. What scripture tells us is that God's timing is always perfect. He will always allow the wind to blow at the perfect time. As a leader, the parallels are obvious.

What are you waiting on?

We are always on the anvil; by trials God is shaping us for higher things. (Henry Ward Beecher)

Nautical Chart

I chose three biblical characters to consider for this concept of patience.

Noah was righteous in God's eyes—God found favor in him. God had decided to flood the Earth and spare Noah and his family. Scripture outlines how God directed Noah to build the ark. I'm sure Noah endured ridicule while he was building the ark on dry land. That took patience. He was then blessed with forty luxurious days and nights aboard the ark with a bunch of stinky animals. That also took patience.

Elizabeth was told she would, in her old age, bear a son. Her husband, Zechariah, didn't believe it, so God told him he wouldn't be able to speak until the baby was born. I'm sure that tested his patience.

Several chapters in his story speak to Moses's needing to be patient. He was incredibly patient with Pharaoh when he refused to let the Israelites go. He was also patient with the Israelites when they left Egypt. They did a lot of griping about a lot of things, and Moses needed patience.

Surely you have experienced a period in life when you were called to wait. Consider their stories and the following questions.

1. What words come to mind?
2. What emotions show up for you in this space?
3. What connections can you draw to your own life story?
4. Do you identify with one of the people mentioned above?
5. Does considering their stories help you better understand some aspect of patience?

Wait patiently for the Lord. Be brave and courageous.
Yes, wait patiently for the Lord. (Psalm 27:14 NLT)

To answer before listening—that is folly and shame.
(Proverbs 18:13 NIV)

On the Water

As a leader, I felt my patience was tested most often when I was forced or obligated to listen intently to someone even though I wasn't necessarily motivated to do so. In communication, patience is required when you find yourself in situations in which you don't want to listen—when you believe what is going to be said has no relevance to anything in the organization or if you simply disagree with the thesis that is being propagated. But to honor, value, and respect the person, and to maintain open communication, which nurtures a climate of dialogue, you listen.

The Color of Paint

He was such a high-maintenance employee. I mean, anytime he had a thought he took it upon himself to find me and make sure I understood his take and vantage point. It didn't matter if we were talking about a leadership team decision or the color of the paint on the wall in the storage shed, he had to weigh in. One morning when I arrived at school, he was standing in the office. His face was red, and he did this thing where he rocked back and forth on the balls of his feet and simultaneously puffed his chest out. When all three were present I knew I needed to really center myself and find the depths of my patience because I was going to need it.

"Well, you're never gonna believe what they did," he began, while he rocked with more velocity.

"Who are *they*? What did *they* do?" I asked, smiling.

"My neighbors—this is the color they are painting their house," he said, handing me a color swatch with an angry, disgusted look on his face. I was speechless. Apparently, the new color, which was sort of a soft canary yellow, was disagreeable.

"I can see this is really bothering you." He was listening. "This isn't something that you can control. It is their house, and you could, maybe, be grateful that they aren't painting it fluorescent green." He chuckled. (I paused.) "I know this is upsetting, but today, right now (looking him in the eye), I need you here for our kids. Those fourth-graders, they need you." (My attempt at the "let it go" speech.) I continued with an idea. "You know, it's really the perfect time of year to paint a house. Temperature is mild, days are longer—more light—maybe you could do something for your neighbor that is … well, outside of the box."

"Mm, like what?"

"Go over there tonight and offer to help paint. I can't imagine that they'd turn you down. I bet in the course of  your conversation you might even get a chance to ask them to reconsider the color." He started nodding his head.

"I have some new rollers I just bought from Home Depot. I'm going to do that." (He said this with a mild look of determination on his face. The rocking continued).

On Monday when he came into work, he stopped in my office, and we greeted each other. He went on to explain that the plan had worked perfectly. He was happy to report that they had reconsidered the color and ended up with a sort of tan, earth tone color that, according to Hank, looked pretty nice.

Yes, this really happened. I did abbreviate the details out of respect for your time. The original conversation was excruciating.

In this situation, I listened for several minutes to an employee who came to work one day and was upset because he just got wind that his neighbors was going to paint their house a color that he found repugnant. All I really did was to demonstrate some patience by listening.

As a leader, you will help people solve personal problems. You will listen, and you will find yourself in the mire of personal stories and situations that are every bit as tantalizing as Hank's paint story, and they may have absolutely nothing to do with their work. But you listen, and you help, and you care because that is what good leaders do. When you are there, remember that your patience in the moment will have a direct impact on the bottom line.

Hank retired about a year after this conversation. As he was leaving, he paid me a very nice compliment. One day we were talking about what he would be doing in retirement, and he thanked me. "You always listened to me, John. I can be kind of ornery sometimes, but you always listened."

First Mate's Log

Principle #12

Patience ... Round #2

If the wind isn't blowing, then the captain of a sailboat simply must roll up his sails and wait for better conditions. It can be frustrating to be out on the water and have the wind quit. Plans change; our patience is tested, and in those situations, we learn to wait. Similarly,

when these situations correlate to God, we often grow impatient with God when we want something to happen. But isn't waiting on His timing always worth it? Right now, He may very well just be waiting for the right conditions to move you forward! When the wind is calm, the sailor looks for signs: ripples on the

water, flags on the shore, trees—anything that shows the wind is moving. When we are in a spirit of waiting, we pray, and we wait, and we pray, and we wait ... looking for signs that God is at work. All the while knowing that God has everything perfectly scripted. His timing is always perfect.

Are you presently in a season of waiting?

> ## "God's delays are not God's denials."
>
> ## —Robert H. Schuller

But those who hope in the LORD will renew their strength. They will soar on wings like eagles; they will run and not grow weary; they will walk and not be faint. (Isaiah 40:31 NIV)

Not only so, but we also glory in our sufferings, because we know that suffering produces perseverance; perseverance, character; and character, hope. (Romans 5:3–4 NIV)

Hope in the LORD and keep his way. He will exalt you to inherit the land; when the wicked are destroyed, you will see it. (Psalm 37:34 NIV)

But do not forget this one thing, dear friends: With the Lord a day is like a thousand years, and a thousand years like a day. The Lord is not slow in keeping his promise, as some understand slowness. He is patient with you, not wanting anyone to perish, but everyone to come to repentance. (2 Peter 3:8–9 NIV)

Nautical Chart

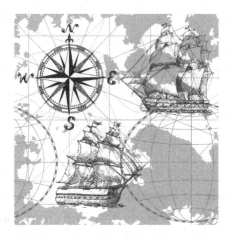

This is round two with patience. I want to focus on one concept that flows through these ideas of being patient and waiting on God: the idea of being exalted.

If you are following God's will for your life, His intention is to exalt you at the proper time. The God of the universe has chosen you to be lifted to participate in the advancement of His kingdom work, and all you must do is sit tight for a moment. Let's end this principle here and quietly consider being exalted by God. It's worth waiting for.

On the Water

There is an adage in leadership I was introduced to many years ago: "Delegate or die." In other words, if you don't figure out a way to use your employees and the gifts and talents they bring to the table, you will die and never realize the potential of your organization. In terms of working with humans, having the patience to develop skills and raw talent into high-flying innovators takes time. The work is methodical and will require a heightened level of patience at every turn.

I have had several employees over the years come to me with raw talent that needed honing, and when that happened, they moved on to bigger challenges and greater opportunities. One employee I will never forget—let's call her Mel. She came to me early in my career. She was a bubbly, highly intelligent employee who had a knack for creativity and engagement. She worked well with people and always had a positive attitude. Her ideas were amazing, and she even did a decent job of planning strategically, which is unusual for a person so young. Her weakness, though, was revealed anytime someone wanted to ask a question or offer constructive refinement of an idea. When that happened, she lost control of her emotions. She would shut down, become quiet, and for anyone willing to engage with her would freely fill a glass of tears as she lamented how she'd been treated. Working with her and waiting for her to mature was killing me. It took an incredible amount of discipline to remain in a coaching stance, but that position eventually helped her overcome her lack of confidence, which really was at the heart of her reaction.

One day when we were debriefing one of her episodes, I asked her where she thought her insecurity came from. She looked at me in a confused sort of way and asked, "You think I'm insecure?" I then revealed how many brilliant things she had come up with in the last year. I listed them. I noted how she had reacted to the thoughts, ideas, and questions that had been offered as those ideas were being presented, highlighting her insecurity—her heightened emotional responses—her shutting down—crying ...

> **In terms of working with humans, having the patience to develop skills and raw talent into high flying innovators takes time.**

"In those moments, it's like you think they are criticizing you," I said.

"Aren't they criticizing me? I mean that's what it feels like. No matter what I say, they find fault."

I responded by reframing the comments. "They are not finding fault; they are trying to deepen their understanding. They are not criticizing; they are clarifying. They are not being negative; they are affirming. Mel, you are in the role as the leader when you present. You are the one with the idea. You are the coach, and when you step before them, you should want their questions. You should want their feedback, and you should want their comments; that's called synergy.

These people are following you. Their questions, clarifications, and comments are strengthening the very structure you built. Can it get any more beautiful?"

She was in tears at this point, but they were not tears from anything negative. She broke through a wall that day. A couple of days later, she led another meeting and killed it. She engaged the questions, thanked them for comments, and climbed the ladder of clarification with a few staff members. It was incredibly positive. We had a moment alone after that meeting, and I asked her how she felt. "Amazing!" was her response. And the look on her face told the whole story.

Patience with employees as they learn and grow can be exhausting. But moments like this remind us how important our work with people is. When we lead from the heart, we commit ourselves to working with people exhaustively and never giving up. When we do this, the mountaintop experiences, like the one I had with Mel, begin to happen more and more often.

> When we lead from the heart, we commit
> ourselves to working with people
> exhaustively and never giving up.

First Mate's Log

Principle #13

The Motorboat and the Sail

Since wind cannot be controlled by humans and must simply be accepted for what it is, many helmsmen prefer the mechanical power of an engine. It is far more comfortable to feel the personal control that comes from the sheer power of a motorized boat. Not having to rely on external forces, the individual is free to determine the course. With a motorboat there is no need for wind. There is no threat of being

motionless due to lack of wind, only the propelling of oneself forward—following one's own plan. This symbolism connects to our life and journey with God. The motorboat in us rejects the supremacy of God. Doing so can move us into hazardous territory, can't it? Individuals who steer their life intent on control motor through life's waters guzzling gas and frequently putting themselves in harm's way. Yielding to the sovereignty of God requires us to let go of control and let the wind do the work.

In what areas of your life are you trying to motor through?

Nautical Chart

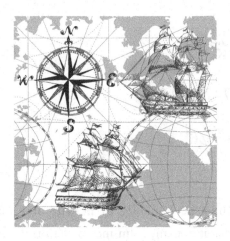

As we consider the motorboat within us, one word that comes to mind—pride. When we go at it alone, it is as if we are stating to the world, "I am all I need." To admonish our own intellect and depend on it solely is to be filled with pride.

I would contend that in leadership, failure always contains an element of pride. When I did a web search of "Bible verses related to pride," I came across a site that lists one hundred verses dealing with the topic! God took this one seriously.

Here are my top ten Bible verses that deal with pride:

1. When pride comes, then comes disgrace, but with humility comes wisdom. (Proverbs 11:2 NIV)

2. But he gives more grace. That is why scripture says, "God opposes the proud, but gives grace to the humble." (James 4:6 NIV)

3. Before a downfall the heart is haughty, but humility comes before honor. (Proverbs 18:12 NIV)

4. Let someone praise you, and not your own mouth; a stranger, not your own lips. (Proverbs 27:2 NLT)

5. For by the grace given me I say to every one of you: Do not think of yourself more highly than you ought, but rather think of yourself with sober judgement, in accordance with the faith God has distributed to each of you. (Romans 12:3 NIV)

6. To some who were confident of their own righteousness and looked down on everyone else, Jesus told this parable: 'Two men went up to the temple to pray, one a Pharisee and the other a tax collector. The Pharisee stood by himself and prayed: 'God, I thank you that I am not like other people— robbers, evildoers, adulterers—or even like this tax collector. I fast twice a week and give a tenth of all I get.' "But the tax collector stood at a distance. He would not even look up to Heaven, but beat his breast and said, 'God, have mercy on me, a sinner.' "I tell you that this man, rather than the other, went home justified before God. For all those who exalt themselves will be humbled, and those who humble themselves will be exalted." (Luke 18:9–14 NIV)

7. Therefore pride is their necklace; they clothe themselves with violence. (Psalm 73:6 NIV)

8. The Lord tears down the house of the proud, but he sets the widow's boundary stones in place. (Proverbs 15:25 NIV)

9. If you think you are standing strong, be careful not to fall. (1 Corinthians 10:12 NIV)

10. In fact, people who think they know so much don't know anything at all. (1 Corinthians 8:2 CEV)

Which verses spoke to you?

As you read the verses, notice the frequency of three words: pride, humility, and wisdom. Do you see the connection between them? The three words produce an interconnected relationship having both great promise and great dread. Leadership that remains humble will be adorned with wisdom. Leadership that violates the rules of humility will fail. It is not a question of *if* but *when*. Perhaps this is why the Bible is filled with passages from both the Old Testament and the New Testament speaking to this end.

The pride battle is something that will show up just about every day in some shape or form. Some examples are taking all the credit, believing too much in yourself and not enough in those around you, and having a conceited attitude about who you are and what you've done.

On the Water

The captain of a large oceangoing ship looked through his telescope into the dark night and saw a light off in the distance. The light was unwavering, not moving left or right. Upon noticing this, the captain feared it was an enemy ship. To determine the light's origin or affiliation, he immediately told his signalman to send a message, "Alter your course ten degrees south."

He promptly received a reply, "Alter your course ten degrees north."

The captain became agitated. He had another idea. In his agitation he sent another message, "Alter your course ten degrees south. I am a captain!"

Soon another reply was received: "Alter your course ten degrees north. I am a third-class seaman."

Now infuriated that someone of a lower rank would be so indignant, the captain stood tall and ordered another message: "Alter your course ten degrees south. I am a battleship."

The reply was, "Alter your course ten degrees north. I am a lighthouse."

At this moment can you think of analogies to your own leadership or perhaps the leadership of others?

Consider the following quotes as you ruminate on the issue of pride.

The Duke of Wellington once haughtily drew himself up to his full height and thundered to one of his staff officers, "God knows I have many faults, but being wrong is not one of them!" The egotistical leader blames mistakes on others, justifies them as inevitable, or refuses to acknowledge them. Because of arrogance, ignorance, or a little of both, leaders start taking shortcuts that compromise their values. In their conceit, they think they're above the rules or are too smart to get caught.

There is perhaps not one of our natural passions so hard to subdue as pride. Beat it down, stifle it, mortify it as much as one pleases, it is still alive. (Benjamin Franklin)

As flawed human beings, we all fall into prideful traps from time to time. However, failing to recognize the error of pride and change course will doom our leadership. Pride is a fatal character flaw and leaders that leave legacies have their character intact. Leaders who fail to prune their pride will meet demise. That's not a guess, it's a guarantee. With pride, it's not a matter of "if" we will fall, but "when." There are no exceptions. (John Maxwell)

The higher you climb, the heavier you fall. (Vietnamese proverb)

The proud person always wants to do the right thing, the great thing. But because he wants to do it in his own strength, he is fighting not with man, but with God. (Soren Kierkegaard)

Pride must die in you, or nothing of Heaven can live in you. (Andrew Murray)

Pride is the mother of arrogance. (Toba Beta)

Write your *pride* story here.

First Mate's Log

Principle #14

The Companionway

In the center of most sailboats is a door of sorts—an entryway—called the companionway. The companionway leads to the cabin,

which can be considered the hub for socializing. It's an area of the vessel where fellowship is unmasked, and crew members can sit down and break bread. It provides a space to rest and take momentary shelter from the weather.

The Bible talks a lot about fellowship with other Christians and its importance for spiritual growth.

As you consider your faith journey, are you lacking an aspect of fellowship?

> They devoted themselves to the apostles' teaching
> and to fellowship, to the breaking of bread and to
> prayer. (Acts 2:42 NIV)

For where two or three gather in my name, there am
I with them. (Matthew 18:20 NIV)

Because of your partnership in the gospel from the
first day until now. (Philippians 1:5 NIV)

And let us consider how we may spur one another on
toward love and good deeds, not giving up meeting
together, as some are in the habit of doing, but
encouraging one another—and all the more as you
see the Day approaching. (Hebrews 10:24–25 NIV)

Nautical Chart

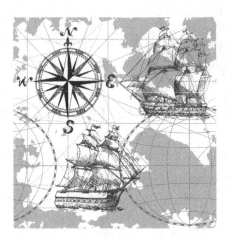

Jesus encouraged us to gather. "For where two or three gather
together as my followers, I am there among them," he states
in Matthew. There is an obvious reason for His direction—
encouragement! Jesus knew the road through life would be hard,
lonely at times, and filled with challenges and conflict, especially as

the gospel is brought forth into the world. His word speaks to the peace that is manifested in each believer as they are drawn together. Each bringing his or her own gifts into a space for all to benefit.

Jesus, who really was the master CEO, understood synergy and the positive effect it can have on a group of people. The collective energy of a few focused people can accomplish anything. We need to remember this as we lead. The failure to invite people into the arena of thinking, debate, planning, and visioning could be the

"For where two or three gather together as my followers, I am there among them."

beginning of pride. You will always do better in partnership with key team members than you ever will on your own.

A second ideal worth mentioning in this section is one that has more of an emotional tenet. I'm speaking to the balance brought to us by interaction with others—and what it can do for the soul. When we interact with people and engage in socializing that exudes an element of fun, we reenergize.

I realize that some will read this and think: "That's not me. I don't like crowds and groups. I prefer to be alone." I would offer this thought: Togetherness doesn't necessarily connote being in a group or large gathering. All humans need interaction. There are times in all our lives, regardless of introversion or extroversion, when people help us. You might be one who is energized by the large party, or you might be one who considers that venue and panic ensues. Instead of a large party, you prefer a quiet cup of coffee or Diet Coke with your closest friend. Either way, you are gathering for the purpose of synergy and garnering energy and power and strength from someone who adds value to your life. In that place, you find your companionway.

On the Water

I met Pastor G on a cold winter day in 1998 at the China Buffet in Albert Lea, Minnesota. Our introduction to one another was very informal—I believe we interacted for only a moment on our way to and from the buffet line. I think we both have slightly different accounts of the words that were exchanged in that meeting.

A few months later, we found ourselves participating in the same community event. As the evening began to wind down, we began a conversation that lasted the better part of three hours. We conversed about life and ministry and who we were as people—we really got to know each other. I felt an instant connection with him that evening and wondered immediately if God might have bigger plans for us.

At that time in my life, I was playing music with another member of the community, and as a duo we were really hoping to find a third member that could do the brunt of the singing. That night I heard Pastor G sing and knew immediately he was the guy. I guess I just needed God to convince him of that as well. Within a week we had a chance to share our music idea with him, and he was really excited to sign on and join the group. Over the course of the next two years, the three of us formed a nonprofit ministry and released two records, played many shows throughout the Midwest, did several radio interviews, and even shared the national stage with a couple of up-and-coming artists. The time I spent with him was a blessed gift, and I came to learn in the months that would pass just how important his friendship was. Some twenty years have gone by since that first meeting, and I can honestly say that he is one of my best friends. I speak with him often—sometimes to joke around and sometimes to talk about ministry and leadership. He is a confidant when I need him to listen, a brother when I need reprimanding, a counselor when I need advice, and a comedian when I need a laugh. All of us should be so lucky to have a Pastor G in our lives.

Finding trusted allies with whom you can swap war stories is a necessary element of effective leadership. Who do you trust? Who is in your corner ready to listen and advise?

So, wherever I am, there's always Pooh,

There's always Pooh and Me.

"What would I do?" I said to Pooh, "If it wasn't for you?"

And Pooh said: "True, it isn't much fun for one, but two, can stick together," says Pooh, says he. "That's how it is," says Pooh.

First Mate's Log

Principle #15

Waiting for God

Ultimately, sailing requires a sailor to adapt to what is presented. Sailors become experts at learning acceptance and at working with what is before them. They have learned to respond to the world as it is and spend little time wishing for something different.

> The sailor must simply accept the wind's bidding and blessings, this way and that, shifting directions, somewhat unexpectedly. The good sailor is accepting that a good strong breeze, can suddenly grow becalmed, only to stir again. This is especially the case in the sultry summer days when the prevailing winds are less evident, and the strength and direction of the winds can be very local, and very subtle. (Author unknown)

Believers must accept this from God, too. There are moments when we must ponder the circumstances that God allows into our lives. When things don't seem to go the way that we want them to, oftentimes we don't readily accept the circumstances. In these scenarios, we need to learn to let God carry us. We must learn to accept God's will.

What circumstances are you pondering right now?

> But those who hope in the LORD will renew their strength. They will soar on wings like eagles; they will run and not grow weary; they will walk and not be faint. (Isaiah 40:31 NIV)

> But as for me, I watch in hope for the LORD, I wait for God my Savior; my God will hear me. (Micah 7:7 NIV)

> Be still before the LORD and wait patiently for him; do not fret when people succeed in their ways, when they carry out their wicked schemes. (Psalm 37:7 NIV)

> Wait patiently for the LORD. Be brave and courageous. Yes, wait patiently for the LORD. (Psalm 27:14 NIV)

Nautical Chart

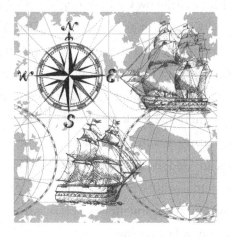

As I surveyed the preceding verses and read through them in different translations, I identified themes relating to this idea of waiting on God. Let's explore.

As we wait, a spirit of peace should invade our souls. We should not be in a state of questioning what God is up to or if He has forgotten about our plight or circumstance—we should be at peace. The peace we exude is a confidence that we have in God to do exactly what He said that He would do. This confidence we place in His omniscience is trust—we trust God. Courage is made manifest in our situations when we have this trust, this peace, this confidence. Trust, peace, confidence, courage—all four working in an interconnected fashion to augment His will for our lives.

For most humans, this process is not easily mastered. Many of us simply are not cut out to wait. The process of waiting is something to perfect, and the formula of waiting is a beautiful thing to behold. Perhaps you've had the opportunity to wait on God, all along knowing His timing was going to be perfect. When I look back over the course of my career and reflect on transitions throughout my journey, I stand amazed at how God's timing was always perfect. Oh, there were times I wished things would move faster! At times it was agonizing, but I reminded myself of these principles repeatedly, and it helped. As I consider just my career journey, I have unrestrained gratitude and wonder what would have happened if my course had been altered by a month, a week, or in some cases, even a day or a few hours. My journey was perfectly timed.

We can rest in God and His promises to do exactly what He said He will do, and it will be perfectly timed. So, put your sails up and pray God will fill them and move you forward according to His divine purpose and in His timing.

On the Water

Managing, coaching, and working directly with people is my favorite part about working in leadership. The camaraderie that comes from developing a family feel around the work we do together is great. But working with people also has its challenges. Sometimes, staff will act in ways that are unkind to one another, sometimes even disrespectful, and when that happens, you usually must intervene.

Each fall, we had a leadership team meeting, and during our

dialogue one year, a staff member made a disrespectful comment about the kids that he was working with. He used a condescending name to describe them, and his comment was not received well. As a new leader, I knew I had to say something. His comment went directly against the ground rules we had established for our work family, so it needed attention.

When we handle delicate conversations with staff members, our movement into those meetings must be strategic. If we don't handle the parameters of the conversation and consider all the variables (mood, tone, feel, present emotional state, current realities, time of day, race, gender, culture) our attempts can fail, and failure in personal space can have far-reaching consequences. It's in these types of situations that grudges, and sometimes deep-seated resentment, are formed. It's extremely difficult to uproot this degree of negativity when it takes hold.

That evening I waited on God and knew that I had to attend to the variables noted above. When would be a good time of day to talk with him? Where should I do that? My office? His classroom? How is he doing emotionally? Will he be able to listen? Is there anything about his current reality I need to be aware of? A couple more days went by, and I was still waiting. It was actually a few weeks before I had what I felt was the perfect circumstance to talk with him. He came in over the Christmas holiday to do some work, and that day, noting that I was there as well, he offered the opportunity to grab a hamburger together. I accepted, and we sat down around noon and had lunch. During our conversation I had an opportunity to mention the leadership meeting, which was now over a month ago, and the condescending comment that was spoken and how it made other people feel.

In the beginning of our conversation, he began sharing some of his frustrations and misgivings—areas in which he felt he could do better. He communicated appreciation for how I had handled some of his errors. In so doing I sensed an authentic desire to do better. It was then that I was able to share. He listened and was honestly appreciative. Our meeting ended that day, and the level of respect that we had for one another grew immensely; he became a trusted ally. A couple of years after my departure from the building, he became the leader in a school.

In this story, I had honestly considered having this conversation several times, but it just didn't feel right. I did second-guess myself a couple of times wondering if I was waiting because I was trying to avoid conflict (a reality for some; be attuned to your own level of fear and conflict avoidance). In the end, I know I was waiting for the perfect time. God's timing is always perfect, and in this case, He proved it.

> When we handle delicate conversations with staff members, our movement into those meetings must be strategic. If we don't handle the parameters of the conversation and consider all the variables (mood, tone, feel, present emotional state, current realities, time of day, race, gender, culture) our attempts can fail, and failure in personal space can have far-reaching consequences. It's in these types of situations that grudges, and sometimes deep-seated resentment, are formed. It's extremely difficult to uproot this degree of negativity when it takes hold.

First Mate's Log

Principle #16

The Fragility of Sailboats

Sailboats are easily tossed about by the slightest of storms and gusts, and yet, in masterful hands, they can maneuver the roughest of waters. Humans are fragile creatures. Many of us are broken and

hurting. Our souls are downcast; easily tossed this way and that by the storms of life. Many of us have little resilience to combat the wars raging inside us, yet amid our brokenness we all have incredible potential to

accomplish greatness. A good skipper can guide a sailboat through any storm. In similar fashion, Christ can guide us through any storm life can muster. His Word will help us maneuver the trials and tribulations that the storms of life create.

What storms are you weathering now that need your undivided attention? Have you given it to the Good Skipper or are you trying to motor through?

I have told you all this so that you may have peace in me. Here on Earth, you will have many trials and sorrows. But take heart, because I have overcome the world. (John 16:33 NIV)

For I can do everything through Christ who gives me strength. (Philippians 4:13 NIV)

Nautical Chart

Take a moment and identify the components of your work that cause you distress. I mean middle of the night, keeping you awake, sick to your stomach fears and preoccupations kind of stress. Write the top three down.

1.
2.
3.

I'm guessing a constellation of emotions came up for you as you considered the impact these situations have had on your life. All leadership encounters storms from time to time. Again, it really isn't a matter of *if* but *when*; it happens to all of us.

Let's delve into this reality for a moment. I want to underscore the veracity with which these storms enter our lives. They are real and they are big. They impact thought, emotions, ability to reason, our health, our families. I even say they run counter to the embodiment of the fruits of the spirit. Of most significance is the human element that is prevalent in all leadership stories that can produce gut-wrenching levels of conflict—wreaking havoc on even the strongest of people.

As we consider our response, our defense, our resolve, let's lean into the fortitude and strength of who we are in Christ. (Rest here for a moment.)

A concept I believe has merit within this principle is, "The David Syndrome"—a Godly confidence that comes over us when we are amid incredibly challenging circumstances. This kind of confidence cannot be explained or understood in human terms because it defies human logic. When the David Syndrome takes effect we respond, think, and act in full knowledge that God's strength is perfect. We *know* God will allow us to overcome whatever is before us. It's the confidence David had in facing Goliath; that same confidence is available to us. When the storms of life beat against us—the wind in our face, driving rain, the ship being tossed from side to side—we have an inner strength—*Christ's strength.*

On the Water

Many times in my life, I perceived leaders as being superhuman. One of the leaders I worked for early in my career was a tall, strong man who never seemed to experience any type of negative emotion. It seemed he could handle any storm that came his way. I saw him forge through conflict, through budget issues, through personal struggles. Publicly he always maintained a confident, strong, peaceful front.

One day I was working late, and I was in the office making a few photocopies. The room was dark, and I overheard him talking on the phone. The tone of his voice was something I hadn't heard before. He was speaking softly, and his voice was cracking. I was hearing deep, raw emotion. I began to walk in the direction of his office when I heard him say, "We all love you and are cheering for you." Just as I turned the corner to enter the office, I saw him hanging up the phone.

"Hi, Will," I said in a sort of unassuming voice.

"Hello, John. Working late tonight?" he said as he reached for a Kleenex. At this point the fact that his phone call had activated some big emotions was an understatement.

"Will, everything okay?"

He paused and looked down. "Sometimes this work is just so

hard," he said in a quiet voice. "That was Joy's husband. They just found out today that she has cancer, and it doesn't look good." He had tears in his eyes, and for the first time I saw his fragility, his humanness.

A few days later we gathered for a staff meeting. We were having a staff breakfast as the holidays were drawing near. He stood before the staff and thanked them for their work. He also talked about how blessed and lucky we were as a staff to have each other. Then he paused and with a broken voice and tears in his eyes, he said, "And let's think about Joy. She is going to need us in the months to come."

If you were to scan the room at that moment, you would have observed the hidden blessings of being fragile. The room was filled with love and people that cared about Joy. She was part of the family that Will was leading. She was one of us.

To be fragile is to be human. It is inevitable that we will encounter situations that expose our emotions and humanity. It's a powerful thing for those you lead to see that side of you—your fragility. It's liberating for many because by simply showing your humanity you validate their emotions, telling them that it's okay to feel—and feel deeply.

First Mate's Log

Principle #17

Below the Waterline

Sailboats are guided by a simple principle of physics. More weight is required below the waterline than above the waterline. The keel of the sailboat is generally in the center of the vessel and extends well below the waterline. The keel holds a significant amount of weight, which stabilizes the sailboat. Dr. David Jeremiah told the story of a sailor who spent time building an incredible sailboat. Its detail was something to behold. Nothing was spared. The interior was incredibly ornate—beautiful wood, exquisite detail. When the boat was put to sea it was done so with great fanfare. A few days later the captain was missing and so was the boat. It was found capsized in the ocean. The craftsman who built the ship spent all his energy on making the ship the best it could be—above the waterline. He attended wonderfully to everything, but he ignored the keel. It wasn't attached properly and likely didn't hold nearly the weight needed to stabilize the boat. When the boat was found—the keel was no longer attached.

Figuratively, our souls are below the waterline. They are easily ignored until the storms of life arise. Our souls need tending in all kinds of weather. Reading scripture, meditating on scripture, memorizing scripture, praying, and surrounding ourselves with other believers—all strengthen our souls and need to be part of our daily routine. These disciplines provide stability and strength—below the waterline.

Is there anything below the waterline that needs attention in your life?

> All have sinned and fall short of the glory of God.
> (Romans 3:23)

Nautical Chart

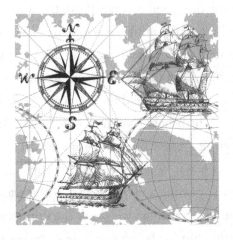

Sin is a tough word, isn't it? It is politically unpopular. It isn't talked about much in churches, and in our culture today we have an affinity for assigning arbitrary weight to values. Much of the time this is determined by the intellectual and academic elite. We live in a morally relative society.

Romans 3:23 states: "All have sinned and fall short of the glory of God."

That means you, that means me. All ... not some, *all!* When I think of falling short, the first idea that shows up for me is this idea of sin. Decisions I have made, things I have done (or not done) that are displeasing to God. As we ponder the "waterline" let's consider what we've done that is displeasing to God.

> **"We are all apprentices in a craft where no one ever becomes a master."**
>
> **—Ernest Hemingway**

We simply cannot enter a consideration of our sin without stopping to consider our heart and our soul. From a spiritual point of view, a malnourished heart is likely to participate in things that displease God. That line of thinking suggests that to avoid acting and thinking in ways that displease God, we need to maintain a steady, healthy spiritual diet.

Stating the importance of maintaining spiritual health is easy; following through is another story. Too often, life gets in the way. Distractions always seem to be present, don't they?

I don't think very many believers would disagree with what has been written here. As I write this, though, I am plagued by one thought. Making the statement that there are distractions in life that prevent us from strengthening our hearts is easy, but it is more complicated than that. There is a force that runs contrary to God, and that force looks for every opportunity to sidetrack you. It is cunning in its pursuit to distract you from knowing God. It wants to divert your attention and starve you to the point where sin takes root—resulting in saying, doing, acting, and believing things that are displeasing to God. The battle is very real.

Take a moment and reflect on your journey. When you consider the idea that a malnourished heart will run counter to the things of God, what shows up for you? What emotions come forth? Does it break you? Does it take you to things you have said, attitudes you've taken, actions you regret? Can you see during those times when you struggled with discipline that sin was right there in words, thoughts, and deeds? Most of the time, these things are happening below the waterline.

For the second time in this log, I have included a Top Ten list of verses. The idea of "our heart" shows up a lot in scripture. God must have thought it was particularly important. As you read, notice how many of the ideas expressed in the verses happen below the waterline.

Top Ten List—Getting to the Heart of It All

1. Do not copy the behavior and customs of this world, but let God transform you into a new person by changing the way you think. Then you will learn to know God's will for you, which is good and pleasing and perfect. (Romans 12:2 NLT)

2. We demolish arguments and every pretension that sets itself up against the knowledge of God, and we take captive every thought to make it obedient to Christ. (2 Corinthians 10:5 NIV)

3. Finally, brothers and sisters, whatever is noble, whatever is right, whatever is pure, whatever is lovely, whatever is

admirable—if anything is excellent or praiseworthy—think about such things. (Philippians 4:8 NIV)

4. For the word of God is alive and active. Sharper than any double-edged sword, it penetrates even to dividing soul and spirit, joints and marrow; it judges the thoughts and attitudes of the heart. ... It is able to judge the thoughts and intentions of the heart. (Hebrews 4:12)

5. For it is with your heart that you believe and are justified, and it is with your mouth that you profess your faith and are saved. (Romans 10:10 NIV)

6. I have hidden up your word in my heart, that I might not sin against you. (Psalm 119:11 NIV)

7. As water reflects the face, so one's life reflects the heart. (Proverbs 27:19 NIV)

8. For it is from within, out of a person's heart, that evil thoughts come—sexual immorality, theft, murder, adultery, greed, malice, deceit, lewdness, envy, slander, arrogance and folly. All these evils come from inside and defile a person. (Mark 7:21–2 NIV)

9. For where your treasure is, there your heart will be. (Matthew 6:21 NIV)

10. I will give them an undivided heart and put a new spirit in them; I will remove from them their heart of stone and give them a heart of flesh. Then they will follow my decrees and be careful to keep my laws. They will be my people, and I will be their God. But as for those whose hearts are

devoted to their vile images and detestable idols, I will bring down on their own heads what they have done, declares the Sovereign Lord. (Ezekiel 11:19–22 NIV)

On the Water

One of the reasons people go to church is to feel good. The word of truth is meant to convict us of sin in our life, and this might be exactly what we need. Unfortunately, it doesn't feel good.

A man lived alone on an island. One day a group of visitors came to the island and were taking notice of the buildings. One of the visitors pointed to a beautiful structure on a cliff overlooking the entire island—a spectacular piece of architecture.

"What is that building?" asked one of the visitors, captivated by the looks of the structure.

Very proudly, the man who lived on the island stood up straight, smiled, puffed out his chest and said, "That is the church I attend."

Another visitor perked up and pointed in the opposite direction and noticed a tall structure on the other side of the island, seemingly equally captivating. Pointing, he said, "What is that building?"

"That's the church that I used to attend. I stopped going there because it didn't make me happy," replied the island owner.

This story has been told over the years to point to the realization that many of us church hop simply because we aren't happy. Pastors and churches are in a tough spot then, aren't they? It is important

for church leaders to be able to have conversations about the things that are displeasing to God with their congregations. How do they do this and keep people happy? If we are going to be real, it's a subject we can't avoid. Much of this work begins below the waterline.

One truth of leadership is decisions we make deemed in the realm of morality are big decisions. Headlines are filled with stories detailing the improprieties of leaders. Decisions in the arena of morality are often life changing. I've seen significant deviation from a life of integrity on various occasions. I've witnessed the following: affairs, marriages ending, grand larceny, embezzlement, theft, lying, and dishonesty. It's never good. I've seen families, lives, and careers ruined. These ruins tend to begin with a single decision. Time and again, that decision is hidden below the waterline.

A friend of mine told the story of an employee who oversaw monetary transactions for their organization. This person took care of the vending machines and would empty the machines out on a regular basis. After the worker had been doing this for a while, the organization noticed that money was missing. For several weeks in a row the amount taken from the machines was significantly less than what it should have been based on the previous month's and year's deposits. Leaders were baffled. Money was being lost. They decided to place a small camera inside one of the vending machines. The obvious premise was that if someone was taking money, this would be an easy way to find out. And they did.

The consequences for decisions like this can be life changing. In a very short period this person's life was altered significantly. What had been growing below the waterline finally made its way to the surface.

If you are engaged in anything that could be front-page news, stop what you are doing and talk to someone you can trust immediately. Be honest and tell him or her you need help. Let it out and build a plan for rectifying the behavior or choices together. If you are living in the gray, walking the blurred lines of morality, do the same. If you remain alone in the journey, the gray you are living in will continue to get darker. Close your eyes and go there for a moment. Is that really where you want to live?

First Mate's Log

Principle #18
The Rudder and the Tongue

The sailboat is controlled by a rudder and a tiller or wheel that moves the rudder from side to side. The rudder can literally be controlled with two fingers, and yet it steers an entire ship. It can also steer the vessel into danger quite easily. A captain can move a vessel into great danger or safe harbor. With most sailboats it takes very little effort to do either. The same is true with the tongue. It can move a soul into great danger. It can kill, injure, hurt, destroy, defame, alter, depress—the possibilities to do harm are endless. As leaders, the words we select and the topics we choose to converse about all have a ripple effect into the lives of the people that we serve. As leaders, oftentimes the words we speak are held in high regard and thus must be chosen carefully. Due to the mere position that we hold in our organizations, we must always guard our tongue. It can easily steer us into dangerous waters.

Are you in dangerous waters?

> Those who guard their mouths, and their tongues keep themselves from calamity. (Proverbs 21:23 NIV)

Taming the Tongue

Not many of you should become teachers, my fellow believers, because you know that we who teach will be judged more strictly. We all stumble in many ways. Anyone who is never at fault in what they say is perfect, able to keep their whole body in check. When we put bits into the mouths of horses to make them obey us, we can turn the whole animal. Or take ships as an example. Although they are so large and are driven by strong winds, they are steered by a very small rudder wherever the pilot wants to go. Likewise, the tongue is a small part of the body, but it makes great boasts. Consider what a great forest is set on fire by a small spark. The tongue also is a fire, a world of evil among the parts of the body. It corrupts the whole body, sets the whole course of one's life on fire, and is itself set on fire by hell. All kinds of animals, birds, reptiles, and sea creatures are being tamed and have been tamed by mankind, but no human being can tame the tongue. It is a restless evil, full of deadly poison. With the tongue we praise our Lord and Father, and with it we curse human beings, who have been made in God's likeness. Out of the same mouth come praise and cursing. My brothers and sisters, this should not be. Can both freshwater and saltwater flow from the same spring? My brothers and sisters, can a fig tree bear olives, or a grapevine bear figs? Neither can a salt spring produce fresh water. (James 3:1–12 NIV)

Nautical Chart

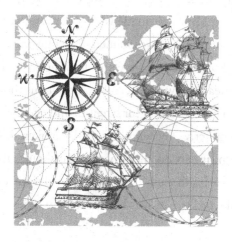

The Power of the Tongue: Two Mice in a Bucket of Cream

A group of mice were milling about the kitchen one day, and two of them accidentally fell into a big bucket of cream. Both mice immediately began swimming trying to avoid drowning in the cream. Although mice are decent swimmers, they soon began to tire. The other mice that had been in the kitchen noticed the two struggling swimmers. They gathered at the edge of the bucket and started yelling at the two mice.

"Just give up," one shouted. "The bucket is too tall; you'll never get out."

One of the mice, hearing the discouraging words simply gave up and died. The other mouse, upon hearing the screams, began to swim harder and faster. Soon he noticed the cream thickening, slowly turning into butter. Before long it was so thick that he was able to walk on top of it and walk right out of the bucket. The moment he reached the other mice, they all cheered.

"Why didn't you just give up when we told you to quit?" one of the mice inquired. "We were telling you to quit, that you would never make it out! But that made you work even harder."

The now freed mouse responded, "Telling me to quit? Oh, I thought the whole time you were encouraging me to keep going."

This story teaches two powerful lessons about the tongue. First, our words hold great promise for strength and encouragement. They can also be destructive. When negativity is spoken to someone who is feeling down, it can do them harm. We should always look for opportunities to build each other up. An elder once said, "If you haven't a kind word to say, it is best to remain quiet."

On the Water

Experiential truths about the words that you speak.

1. It takes roughly ten positive comments or affirmations to make up for one negative comment or put-down.

    a. One of my supervisors used to put people down on a regular basis, and he often did this in meetings. As a result, the climate (remember that one) was awful. People were always looking over their shoulders. Trust was nonexistent, and people were very hesitant to fully engage in the work.

2. If someone feels your words have been harmful, then they *have* been harmful, and there is no debate. It simply doesn't matter what your intent was.

    a. An employee once went out of her way to talk with me about some words I used in conversation with her one day. She did this because she thought I would care. When she explained how she felt, I got defensive and pushed back. She walked away discouraged. I was quite young and inexperienced, but I was fully aware of my mistake. Simply, I should have listened. I went to see her the next day and made amends. There were no excuses.

3. Be slow to speak and long on listening.

    a. As leaders, we are often in situations where we really want to speak and generally have lots to say. It might be in a meeting, conversation, or dialogue about some aspect of work; it might be on the phone or in a video chat. It is important that you deliver your thoughts—your information or opinions—when people are ready to listen. In communication you want to maximize the impact of your ideas. You accomplish this by being long on listening.

4. Praise goes a long way.

   a. We all feel good when we receive praise. This is certainly not a new idea or thought. As a leader, there is a word of caution around the use of praise—a rule if you will. Praise needs to be sincere. If it is not, you will lose credibility as a communicator, and you will erode trust. When you praise, be specific, be detailed—talk of the impact of the work you are observing and conclude the praise with a thank-you.

   b. Several years ago, we were opening a new addition to our school. The grade level that was moving into the new wing spent a great deal of time in the fall of the year preparing the space for kids. Just before we were about to open the doors and invite families in, I gathered them in a circle. We huddled up, and I explained in detail what was so awesome about their work: the color, the creativity, the arrangement of space, "Kids are going to love this!" I said. I went on with more detailed praise. We broke from the huddle and went on with what turned out to be a highly successful open house.

5. Words not carefully chosen can do great harm.

   a. In many forms of communication, we must understand something that I call the continuum of seriousness. The continuum of seriousness speaks to the type of response that is warranted on the part of the receiver. When someone is seeking a casual yes or no, am I on the right track type of answer, the response need not be serious. On the other hand, if the inquirer is seeking a detailed and thoughtful response, a curt answer would not be appropriate.

b. The incorrect response can yield several different emotions on the part of the receiver, and none of them are productive.

> **In communication you want to maximize the impact of your ideas. You accomplish this by being long on listening.**

First Mate's Log

Principle #19

All Lines Are Organized

It was a pristine day for sailing. The wind was just right—not too gusty. I was alone and enjoying some peace—a blissful moment. I had both sails up, and I had just come about, all set to enjoy the sail back to our home. In a split second, everything changed. Unbeknownst to me, the tiller handle was about to free itself from the rudder. I moved the rudder to one side, and the tiller became detached. Immediately the rudder slammed to one side, forcing the boat into a sharp turn, and making it tip to about a sixty-degree

 angle. Intuitively, I uncleatted the mainsail. That single act stabilized everything. The boat leveled off, and I was able to engage the tiller. This all happened in just a moment, but one thing made all the difference. One habit prevented me from capsizing: the organization of my ship. The centerboard block, a type of pulley; the jib lines; the mainsail; and jib halyard lines were all within two feet

of each other, which allowed me to easily control all aspects of the vessel under unforeseen circumstances. On a well-organized sailboat, all lines lead to the cockpit.

What organizational challenges are you facing?

> But everything should be done in a fitting and orderly way. (1 Corinthians 14:40 NIV)

> Go to the ant, you sluggard; consider its ways, and be wise. It has no commander, no overseer or ruler, yet it stores its provisions in summer and gathers its food at harvest. How long will you lie there, you sluggard? When will you get up from your sleep? A little sleep, a little slumber, a little folding of the hands to rest. (Proverbs 6:6–11 NIV)

> Suppose one of you wants to build a tower, won't you first sit down and estimate the cost to see if you have enough money to complete it? (Luke 14:28 NIV)

> Whatever you do, work at it with all your heart, as working for the Lord not for human masters. (Colossians 3:23 NIV)

Nautical Chart

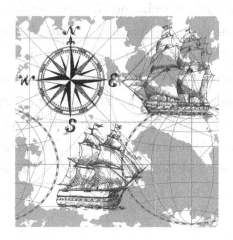

I'm an organized person. I like everything in its place and believe everything has a place. I prefer to operate this way at home, in the office, and on a sailboat. The consequences of being disorganized are many. Angry customers, lessened levels of productivity, and an overall lack of efficiency on an operational and human level all begin with disorganization. Simply, a lack of organization prevents people, systems, and entities from achieving their purpose.

On the Water

In one of my positions, our leader utilized an idea that now transcends the entire organization. We affectionately called it "the three Cs": connection, coherence, and consistency, all of which must be realized at full capacity for an organization to reach a high level of effectiveness. Operationally, "the three Cs" were used frequently, serving as a guide and rubric to gauge and evaluate everything we do. When things didn't progress or meet our performance expectations, "the three Cs" helped us dissect the data. The routinizing of this tool brought our work as a department and an organization to an exceptionally high level of congruence.

First Mate's Log

Principle #20

All Hands on Deck

At times, the sail is simply magical. The winds are perfect; you set the automatic helm to a specific coordinate; you relax in the cockpit and enjoy the company of those aboard. During an emergency, though, everything changes. Maybe it's a sudden weather-related event, a man overboard—an emergency of some kind that requires action on the part of everyone. In leadership, "all hands on deck" means that everyone is doing what they are trained and expected to

do, and if they don't follow through, the team will be in deep doo-doo (please chuckle).

Whether it's a crew on a sailboat or a team within an organization, each member has a job, a set of expectations, a role, and a responsibility to help the team succeed. It is the law of interdependence that ultimately achieves massive success. Team members cannot be successful on their own—teamwork is required.

During an emergency, are all hands on deck?

Two are better than one, because they have a good return for their labor: If either of them falls down, one can help the other up. But pity anyone who falls and has no one to help them up. Also, if two lie down together, they will keep warm. But how can one keep warm alone? Though one may be overpowered, two can defend themselves. A cord of three strands is not quickly broken. (Ecclesiastes 4:9–12 NIV)

Nautical Chart

The acronym TEAM connotes:

T—Together

E—Everyone

A—Accomplishes

M—More

I conducted a search on the topic of teamwork and found a couple hundred thousand posts. Clearly, much has been written on the topic of teamwork and its necessity to accomplish the goals of an organization. I am certain there are many heroic stories attesting to the importance of teamwork, and many of which are quite captivating. I will leave it to the authors of those stories to talk through their versions of teamwork. For this next "On the Water" section, I'll borrow from my own experience. I have dialed into a few principles that accurately govern this notion of all hands on deck.

On the Water

God-centered, God-breathed leadership is inspiring to people. Inspired people change the world. They are far more likely to wander into unknown areas to explore new possibilities. When this happens creativity and ingenuity are unleashed.

Great leaders won't spend their time running around trying to fix what isn't working. Instead, they look for the symptoms of inefficiency and ineffectiveness, and they act to amend the root of the problems. More importantly, great leaders look to God before they look to themselves in all circumstances.

Here's my top ten list.
Everyone on board must:

1. Be absolutely clear regarding their responsibilities.

    a. The beginning might be something as simple as a job description, but that alone rarely defines the key responsibilities for an individual in an organization. Team members should all be able to describe the intricacies of their work and how they impact the larger group.

2. Understand how interdependence is achieved.

    a. Interdependence is the notion that ultimate success happens within the collective work of each team member. For the team to succeed, individuals must succeed. Team members must see their role as necessary and significant and understand how the overall organization is impacted by their work.

3. Have a clear idea of what success looks like.

    a. How is success determined? How will we know when we have achieved success? What metrics help us understand if we are on the right path or veering off the path? Are successive approximations defined and clear?

4. Understand what the reward will be.

    a. Intrinsic rewards are more effective than extrinsic rewards. Many organizations see extrinsic rewards as being a great method for motivating employees, but the research from industrial psychology suggests that they matter little. Years of research has shown us repeatedly that people want to be part of something bigger. A sense of self-worth and accomplishment come from feeling like you are truly contributing to a cause.

5. Understand the *why* behind the work.

   a. Why are we working so hard? Why is this important? Why does it matter?

6. Understand the consequences of failure.

   a. Failure has many consequences including decreased revenue, loss of jobs, diminished organizational vitality, and an overall decrease in organizational effectiveness. A keen awareness of the consequences of failure can help your crew stay focused and accomplish what needs to be done.

7. Understand there is a moral imperative to the work.

   a. It isn't always easy to do this, but attaining a high level of intrinsic motivation is all about establishing a moral imperative—we do this work because it will impact lives. At the beginning of each school year, after our back-to-school staff meeting, I would ask staff to put everything down and give me their undivided attention. It was the same speech most years and went something like this. "On Tuesday, five hundred kids will pass through our doors and head to our classrooms. The kids that come to us all have one thing in common. They need you. They need you desperately. You may well be the only person in their life they can depend on and you, we, need to come through for them. We may be the only hope they have." This yearly speech, as I was told, made an indelible impact on staff as they put the "back-to-school" duties in perspective and focused on the kids. The kids were the moral imperative.

8. Be motivated.

9. See the individuals in the organization as being connected, the work coherent, and the execution of the work consistent.

    a. The three Cs are important in any organization. The work of the organization must be connected, coherent, and consistent. When any one of these breaks down, the entire mechanism has the potential to fail.

10. Care.

    a. The Ford Motor Company manufactured a car in the '70's called the Pinto. It was a subcompact car made in Detroit. It wasn't Ford's best work. After enduring what seemed to be insurmountable problems with overall quality, the company decided to commission a study to determine the source of the problems. They believed that the car was either flawed from a design standpoint or the issues were a result of faulty manufacturing. The result of the study? Hidden cameras on the assembly line told a story of people who simply didn't care and workers who took no pride in their work. In one section of the assembly line, the operators of the lift, a mechanism that lifted the frame of the car up into the air—would drop the car for no apparent reason. From perhaps ten feet in the air, the frame of the car would freefall, hitting the concrete floor below. The noise it would make as it hit the ground was routinely met with laughter. This would happen several times each day. Of course, the deliberate action weakened the frame of the car, which in time, gave way to other mechanical maladies. It's reasonable to conclude that those working on the assembly line did not care deeply about their work.

I would be remiss concluding a section entitled, "All Hands on Deck" without trying, at least momentarily, to capture the idea of synergy. As with the concept of teamwork, the internet is replete with examples of what this looks like in the workplace. Again, I will leave it to the writers of these examples to debate the ins and outs of synergy as my experience in leadership frames its own definition.

Synergy is the collective power of the team uniting for a common purpose. When the forces, the intellect, the passion, the gifts, and the character of your organization gather collectively around the mission, incredible things happen.

First Mate's Log

Principle #21

Man Overboard

No situation aboard a sailboat challenges the crew more than a man overboard (MOB). In that moment, all the variables that make up an experienced helmsman are put to the test. At the call, *"Man overboard,"* the crew immediately initiates a series of procedures to bring the person back aboard. The protocol goes like this:

Y—Yell

Yell to alert the crew that a man is overboard.

T—Throw

Throw a type IV life vest or any other buoyant device toward the MOB.

P—Point

One of the crew members continues to point to the MOB so that the rest of the crew knows their location.

S—Set

Set the MOB button in the GPS.

C—Call

Call VHF 16.

As this sequence is set in motion, the helmsman maneuvers the vessel in a figure eight fashion and circles back to come alongside the MOB. Crew members act to accomplish the rescue.

Now turn your thinking toward your organization. What does a team member who has gone overboard look like? Is it an employee  not dialed in to the mission and vision of the company? Someone perhaps who has gone rogue? Is it a misguided skill set or a lack of connection with specific individuals? Whatever the case may be, it is delaying forward movement—progress is being hampered. Instead of focusing on collective synergy, the team is logging minutes rescuing.

Is there a MOB on your ship?

> Be sure you know the condition of your flocks, give careful attention to your herds. (Proverbs 27:23 NIV)

Nautical Chart

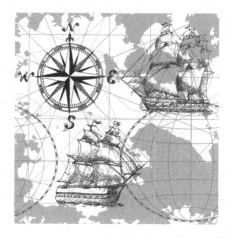

    As the leader, it is incumbent on you to deal with MOBs using the same precision and expertise you would if it were to happen while sailing. The MOB must be addressed because it has great potential for detracting from the bottom line and the overall morale of the organization. Choosing to not deal with the MOB would be compromising many things. Climate will likely be impacted; trust will erode, and your capacity as a leader will ultimately be reduced. A MOB within your organization can elicit strong emotions that will impact staff negatively in a variety of ways.

On the Water

Let's examine a few strategies for addressing the MOB in your organization.

When dealing with a MOB, executing some degree of control over the situation and system is necessary. Your thinking and the mechanisms you use need to be precise. I've noted below some strategies that have served to guide my work over the years.

Suggested Strategies

1. **Know yourself**
   a. Because you are potentially entering into a conflict situation, you need to make sure that you know and understand your own leadership style. How do you handle conflict? How does your body respond to situations that have the potential for being stressful? Are there triggers that make you defensive? Are you attuned to your body language?

2. **Rehearse**
   a. Rehearse the conversation and the various ways the employee might respond. Consider their character,

the emotions they typically exhibit, the tone of voice they use, and the way they respond to criticism or corrective action. Consider every dimension including factors such as race, gender, age—underestimating the impact of these variables in the conversation can lead to catastrophic results.

3. **Set a time to meet**
   a. MOB conversations begin with some degree of formality, and it's best if the employee knows the purpose of the meeting. My suggestion is that a day or so before the meeting you communicate "a desire to discuss some concerns that have arisen." Set a time for the meeting and who will be in attendance. In most situations, the MOB is not surprised by the request, and giving the person a day or more will allow him or her processing time.

      How you communicate this meeting request is equally important. I have had situations where I talked to the person face to face and other situations where I used email. There are occasions in which I used both. You must consider the person, your relationship with that person, and which method will spur the employee to reflect on the situation.

4. **Stick to the facts**
   a. When it comes to sharing the evidence supporting the concern, stick to things that are completely factual. Avoid phrases like, "It seems like ..." or words like, "never," "sometimes" and "always." Evidence is best communicated using exact representation of events.

Quotes, dates, times, and examples where responsibilities were not met—a high level of detail is necessary. Facts allow you to solidify the concern and help to center the conversation and prevent it from being a personal attack. If you can't detail facts, then you must question if there is truly a cause to articulate a concern.

5. **Explain the structure of the conversation**

   a. As you begin the meeting, be clear about the purpose and structure. Here's an example:

      i. "We are meeting today to discuss performance concerns that have arisen over the course of the past two months. I'm going to review those concerns with you, and when I'm done, I'm going to share with you some directives related to the concerns and establish a timeline for improvement. I will also detail for you the support structures we will put in place so you can receive the support necessary to succeed. We need you operating at full capacity. We need your skills, your character, your creativity—we need it all. Our organization gets better when you get better."

6. **Garner a commitment to change**

   a. Once the structure of the meeting is presented, it is time to garner a commitment to change. The MOB will need to commit to listening and improvement. If they are not ready and willing to consider the evidence, then the meeting can end. Continuing without a commitment is pointless. Garnering a commitment can be done in various ways.

Once when I was conducting a MOB discussion, the employee lost control of their emotions—became agitated and very defensive. I promptly ended the meeting and sent the employee home. I stated that having this meeting and sharing these concerns was necessary before returning to work. I communicated I would be rescheduling the meeting. When I had completed the statement, I excused myself and left the employee alone in the room with their union representation. This was done strategically. Their representation helped them understand the necessity of their compliance and the gravity of what took place.

7. **Establish clear outcomes**

    a. Markers of success must be extremely clear. To assure they are clear, consider how they can be measured. Are there timelines that need to be met? Is there a necessary quantity or quality of work? If meeting with someone is required, are the dates and times of those meetings scheduled? The outcomes are part of the remediation plan and need to be clearly understood.

8. **Explain the support structures**

    a. Detail how you will support the MOB in the process to get back aboard. Are there people they need to spend time with? Is there a training module they need to complete? All support to help bring the person back on the ship needs to be communicated clearly. As you work through each of these steps, it is important to confirm understanding.

9. **Determine a follow-up date**

   a. At the conclusion of the discussion, present a follow-up date so the MOB knows that this conversation is not over and that further discussion is necessary.

10. **Entertain Questions**

    a. Allow the MOB to ask clarifying questions.

11. **Remember you are working with a human being**

    a. Circumstances involving employees that are overboard are most definitely some of the most challenging situations that exist in leadership. Middle-of-the-night stress and sleeplessness is often associated with such scenarios. If we really care about people and truly value our employees, then we are going to make a concerted effort to do this right. And it *can* be done right.

Man Overboard—One Story …

She was a seasoned veteran, but as her experience grew, so did her callousness toward humans, especially little humans. She was short with kids, frequently impatient, at times condescending and sarcastic, and this was all happening with increasing frequency.

One day I received a letter from a parent that spoke directly to these concerns and offered another angle by explaining in detail how these behaviors were impacting her daughter. The letter was sent to me, and unbeknownst to me, also to our superintendent and a member of the school board.

I had just finished reading the letter when the phone rang. It was the superintendent, and he was calling to inquire what my thoughts were regarding engaging with the teacher. We conversed for a few minutes. I didn't really feel I needed his help. If anything, I felt his presence in the situation fueled more issues. This teacher was part of my family, and I needed to handle this situation with velvet gloves.

I made a copy of the letter and went to see her when I knew she wasn't with kids. I told her that I, along with the superintendent and school board, had received a copy of the letter. I told her it wouldn't be easy to read, and she needed to take it seriously. I also stated I wanted to schedule a meeting with her and a representative from her union to talk about these concerns. She nodded her head and said that would be okay.

I had about two days to think through how I was going to handle the meeting, what I thought I might encounter from her in terms of defensiveness and emotions, and I wondered how having her union representative present would prevent us from talking honestly about the issues. I took the time I had to prepare.

When the meeting began, I laid out the structure that I intended to follow. I said I had spent time looking over the letter considering what had been communicated, had drawn up some summative statements, and had some suggestions. I then explained I needed to share this without pause or interruption. I let them both know there would be ample time for questions and dialogue, but we would do that later. They both agreed, and I proceeded.

I began: "Here is the letter that we received. It was sent to me, the superintendent, and the school board. I also gave you a copy of the letter. The letter speaks to a few specific examples of things that have transpired in your classroom. You read the letter, so I know you are aware of that. Today, and during this meeting, I don't really want to talk about these specific situations. (She was a bit surprised by this.) I do, however, want to share some thoughts I believe are general perceptions about you, your classroom, and the things you are doing—the words you use, the tone you use, and the way you interact with kids. I want to talk about how kids are feeling (nodding affirmations).

"There is a belief that you are mean to kids. The letter speaks to this, and you know this isn't the first time I have heard this. (She nodded.) The letter also states this student is afraid of you. She's afraid to ask questions and doesn't feel she can approach you. The third observation is that you have been sarcastic and make fun of kids. There is a tone you use with kids—it's a manner that you have—and it isn't perceived as being respectful."

Once I had summarized the larger concerns, I went back and talked about each one individually, and I highlighted dates and times I had experienced the issue.

"Let's talk about the first concern. She feels you are mean to kids. Last week, Pat, you asked me to intervene with those three girls that were having a disagreement on the playground. Remember that? Pat, when I was talking with them, I asked the girls why they didn't just talk with you. They paused for a moment, and one of the girls spoke and said, 'Mrs. K is mean. She wouldn't listen.' Remember the next day Michael was out in the hallway, and I walked by? He was crying, and I asked him what was wrong. The first words out of his mouth were, 'Mrs. K is mean. She doesn't like me.' I can share more but I want to pause and ask you to consider the perception. There is a perception that you are mean to kids." I paused for a moment.

"There is. I mean, they do feel that way, don't they?" She responded softly and had a tear in her eye.

I then went through the next two concern areas and provided examples, dates and times, and exact words that kids and parents spoke, all to inform the concern. Each time Pat nodded in affirmation that what I was saying was hard to refute. (Notice here that I went to great lengths to make sure I wasn't stating an opinion—I let the data talk.) When I was done, I went back and reviewed the three concerns again. I closed my folder and took a breath and centered myself. The room was very quiet but peaceful.

I continued, "Pat, you are an amazing teacher. We have worked together for four years now, and I have seen you do incredible things with kids. (I shared specific examples.) But right now, we are forced to really look at some concerns that have arisen, and these concerns relate directly to how kids feel. And, Pat, I want these to go away so kids can see, know, and experience the teacher you mean to be." Pat was nodding through this. I could tell she felt bad.

"So, the big question is really what are we going to do about this? I have some ideas. Let me share. [Pause] It's time to have a talk with your kids about how they're feeling. Go right into the storm, Pat—let them talk, let them share—accept everything. This will help them feel better immediately."

She was writing this down and nodding her head.

"I also want you to talk to this parent. I'm not going to tell you what to say; just talk to her face to face. Let your heart lead you. I have two more ... ready? They are silly. Still ready? One day a week from now on, I want you to eat lunch with your kids. I can't make you—I just think it would be a good idea."

She nodded here with a touch of dissonance.

"Ready for number two? On another day go to the playground ten minutes early and spend that time interacting with them outside. Better yet, when you go pick them up, tell them you are extending recess by ten minutes. I might warn you, though, the other third-grade teachers may not like you very much."

She was smiling.

"The last thing that I want you to do is just spend some time reflecting."

A moment of silence followed as Pat nodded her head; she said, "okay," a couple of times. Her colleague then spoke up.

"Wow. Wow, John." (Pause. I really didn't know what was coming when she said this.) "This was really positive. This whole thing could have been so mean and hard, and it was just so positive." (Lots of affirmative body language at this moment from both—looking at Pat.) "You got this, Pat, and we're both going to make sure you figure this out. Wow, John. Thank you."

I never saw the response from Pat's colleague coming. But then sometimes that's how God works. We ended the meeting, and the issues went away. Over the course of the next six months, I saw the two of them talking from time to time. I walked into Pat's room a few times within the next few weeks, and there was a different feel. I even caught her on the playground one day. She made some commitments that day to herself and her kids. Those commitments made a difference.

The most challenging times bring us the most empowering lessons. (Karen Salmansohn)

First Mate's Log

Principle #22
A Time to Be Captain

As a principal, I tried to be inclusive when it came to decision making. Whenever we were debating significant decisions that would impact a lot of people, I worked hard to include key stakeholders in the process. Inclusion in leadership was important to me. As I brought people into our organization, I attempted to hire people with an aptitude for things that would benefit our organization. However, in all modes of leadership, there are times when collaboration and shared decision making is held at bay. Let's hit the water!

It seemed to be the perfect day to sail. We got out on the water; sails were up, and we had established a healthy heel. As we sailed along, I happened to glance over my shoulder and noticed a wall of blackness had developed. As I scanned the horizon, I noticed it was moving toward us rather quickly. I read the signs and immediately entered an autocratic mode—spouting directions: life jackets on, furl the jib (roll up the front sail), reef the main (reduce the square footage of the mainsail), secure the galley (secure everything below deck, especially the kitchen area). I stayed calm but needed everyone to know this was not the time for discussion.

There are times in leadership where you will need to do this. Moments where you simply direct people. There isn't time for debate. It's likely these moments will be embedded in something serious where decisiveness is needed. Knowing when to be decisive and when you are being dismissive is critical to the momentum of any leader. Act too quickly, and you will be criticized for being a poor listener; act not at all, and you will be seen as one drowning in the waters of complacency.

Moses ... Remember him? (Read the book of Exodus)

Nautical Chart

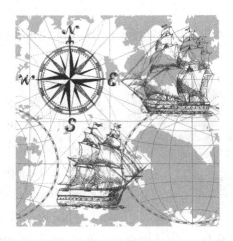

I will admit I did not spend much time researching and considering biblical references for this final principle. However, there are an abundance of poignant leadership scenarios and situations to dissect in the life of Moses. From the moment he relinquished his Egyptian heritage, to leading the Israelites from Egypt, to establishing the Ten Commandments, his story provides a stage to pursue and analyze many leadership constructs.

Two moments of his life rise to the top for me in which he had to be decisive and unwavering in his resolve. The Red Sea on one side and Pharaoh on the other and a bunch of extremely cranky people in the middle—it was time to be decisive. He didn't have anything to say to the Israelites; he wasn't even contemplating negotiating with Pharaoh and his army. He turned to the Red Sea and, resting in God's power, commanded it to comply.

Another moment in his iconic story is when he stood before Pharaoh. "Please let my people go … pretty please." Ah, no … he demanded it! The dialogue was no doubt direct, specific, and left no room to debate potential alternatives. "Let my people go!" These two scenarios illustrate autocracy in the life of a leader who knew when it was time to act.

On the Water

Autocracy is something I always tried to avoid as a leader. I much preferred consensus building over directives. There were times, though, in which I acted in ways that were more autocratic. Those moments generally revolved around the topic of safety. In those situations, I was preoccupied first and foremost with making sure everyone remained safe by following the policies and protocols that had been established for such times.

It was a snowy March day, and the weather forecast called for sixteen inches of snow to fall beginning at 8:00 a.m. and continuing throughout the day. We ended up closing school early that day. Making the decision to close school early may not sound like a monumental decision, but I can assure you that it is. Moving five hundred kids from school safely home in an early release is a huge challenge. When I received the phone call stating that we would indeed be closing early, I moved into autocracy mode. You would have observed me delivering communication, answering questions, defining the movement patterns to and from transportation, directing buses once they began to land, moving kids to crossing corners, helping to maintain calm in the parking lots, and dealing with questions from parents and staff.

You would have seen very little back-and-forth dialogue, no long pauses, or time for wonderment—everything was direct. The goal, of course, was to make sure that kids got home safely. There wasn't room for indecision; it was time to be the captain.

First Mate's Log

Epilogue

As I ponder and ruminate over the symbolism of sailboats as it relates to our journey through this life with Christ, I am astounded. I marvel at the endless connections that can be drawn between the two. When the sails are raised, they fill with wind, and the vessel moves. As the voyage begins, the skipper is prepared to experience a multitude of conditions and situations that will, without question,

force him to react, perhaps intuitively, so that a safe arrival to port is ultimately achieved. From romancing the wind to setting anchor, from tolerating the eb and flow of the tides, to surviving the fiercest gale, the captain always must be ready. Readiness is achieved on various levels as we have seen in *The Captain's Log*. From understanding the equipment, to plotting a course, to knowing the intricacies of the team, to monitoring the landscape—all impact the outcome and the eventual safe arrival at port. The parallels between sailing, our spiritual walk, and work in leadership on this earth are truly remarkable. We ought to think of ourselves as vessels sailing the sea of life with Christ as our helmsman. Doing so will assuredly allow for, one day, a blessed journey home.

SAILS UP 4 HIM

SAILS UP 4 HIM is a nonprofit organization dedicated to leaders of all kinds. As a consultant and leadership coach, I choose to work with my clients on the water. The restoration process used to revive, restore, and review leadership and organizational effectiveness takes place aboard a thirty-foot Catalina MKII sailboat. Leaders usually spend a couple of days on the water, sailing and talking leadership. For these retreats, I use the content embedded in *The Captain's Log* as a tool to encourage dialogue and reflective conversation. If time on the water talking about your leadership and organization sounds interesting and exciting to you, feel free to  contact me at SailsUp4Him@gmail.com. If my consultation services or public speaking might be of interest to you, I welcome an inquiry.

Blessings on your life's voyage,

JP

Appendix A

On Your Voyage ...

As you head out to sea and start sailing, use these questions as a guide and tool for reflection.

Principle #1: The Anchor Holds	• Is your anchor established? • Do you feel anchored? • Do you feel that you have a work/life balance? • How do you spend your time? • We always can find time to do what we want to do. Is it a priority to spend time with God? • How do you center yourself? • What do you look like and sound like when you are not centered? • What tends to mess with your ability to be centered? • Is there one zone (feeling, acting, thinking, believing) that you spend more time in than others? • Can you identify people that have the tendency to move you off center?

Principle #2: **The Cross** **before Us**	• How do you keep the cross before you? • Is this ever something you talk about as a leadership team? • Are you focused organizationally on the cross? • What distracts you from keeping the cross at the center of your life? • How can you neutralize these distractions? • Is your faith allowed at work, or do you leave it at the door? • Do your employees understand your reliance on Christ? • Do you ever feel that you are compromising your faith? • How do you communicate your faith? • How much time is devoted to this each day?
Principle #3: **Plot the Course**	• Do you have a vision for your leadership and organization? • What tools do you use to plot your course? • Are systems aligned to course direction and goals? • Who do you typically involve in planning? • Are there voices and expertise that you purposefully include for decision making? • Are there voices and expertise that you purposely exclude from decision making? • Is your decision-making process transparent? • Is it ever hard for you to be decisive?

	• What indicators exist that suggest that you are off course?
	• Are you overlooking anyone that could be an asset to the process?
Principle #4: Know Your Crew	• Can you articulate the relative strengths and weaknesses of your leadership team?
	• Can you identify people on your team who have a greater aptitude for elements of your work than you do?
	• Do you hire leaders?
	• Do you know how to hire leaders?
	• Who do you invite into the hiring process? Why?
	• How is leadership shared to maximize organizational effectiveness?
	• How do you quantify hiring practices?
	• What is in place that holds the hiring practices accountable?
	• Prior to hiring anyone, do you ever openly discuss the process?
	• Does bias ever enter the process?
	• Would you be able to recognize it if it did?
Principle #5: Know the Signs	• What relative indicators of success are the focus of your leadership team?
	• Are there objective measures in place to evaluate progress and process?
	• What do red flags look like?

	• How do you determine the climate of your organization?
	• Are there measures in place to evaluate climate?
	• What are the primary sources of conflict within your organization?
	• Are specific people routinely associated with conflict?
	• How do you encourage risk taking?
	• How is excellence rewarded?
	• Are there any areas of the organization that don't feel coordinated?
Principle #6: Get in the Boat	• Presently, are there initiatives that you are hesitant to pursue?
	• What is causing the apprehension?
	• What do you have to lose?
	• What is leadership afraid of?
	• Organizationally and from a leadership perspective, what do you fear?
	• What keeps you awake at night?
	• Are there any positives that can be associated with failing?
	• What are the consequences of failing? (Think of something you are hesitant to move on.)
	• How do you bring your faith into these circumstances?
	• Have you ever considered mapping your decisions? (Decision tree concept to work through risk.)

Principle #7: **Communicate** **Your Position**	• What communication vehicles work for you? • Has anyone in your organization given you any feedback regarding communication? • What are your communication strengths? • What are your communication weaknesses? • Are there any team members who can augment your communication routines? • When was the last time you considered a communication audit? • Is there a type of communication that seems to be more effective for you than another? • From your point of view, what are the advantages of the three-by-three rule? • Is there a mode of communication that you feel more comfortable with? • What does your communication system look like?
Principle #8: **Prepare to Come** **About**	• When you consider change, are there specific protocols in place to assure a smooth transition? • How do you assure maximum coordination during change? • What mechanism of communication assures smooth sailing through choppy, change-oriented water? • Are there key people that you communicate with when considering a course change? • How do you calculate the risk of a new initiative?

	• How do you gather input when you are considering change?
	• Your employees have skills and talents. How do you assure that you are using everything available to you?
	• Do you feel that standing on the pier has advantages?
	• Can the change that you are considering be implemented incrementally?
	• Have you ever made it a practice to map out initiatives? What are the advantages and disadvantages of this?
Principle #9: Sense the Wind	• What indications suggest a storm is brewing?
	• How do you read the landscape of your organization?
	• Do you feel like you can sense when things are "off"?
	• What qualitative indicators suggest things are off organizationally?
	• What quantitative indicators suggest things are off organizationally?
	• Who do you trust to give you clues as to the state of the organization?
	• How does your faith enter this process of sensing the wind?

	• Are there things that you can do to increase your sensitivity to God?
	• How does God talk to you?
	• Is there anyone in your organization who you trust that can guide you in this area?
Principle #10: The Holy Spirit and the Wind	• Do you ever pray for the manifestation of the Holy Spirit to be revealed in your work and leadership?
	• Is there a strong spiritual presence in your leadership and organization?
	• How do you know if the Holy Spirit has filled your sails?
	• How does this aspect of faith enter your organization and work?
	• Does the idea of the Holy Spirit make you uncomfortable?
	• Organizationally, what indicates that your sails are luffing?
	• On the top of the mast is an apparatus called a windex. It shows from what direction the wind is blowing and serves as a tool that helps guide the vessel. Is there a comparable apparatus within your organization?
	• How does God play a role in big decisions?
	• How do you listen to God?
	• How does God speak to you?

Principle#11: Patience	• Now, what are you waiting on?
	• Do you ever experience impatience because of having to wait?
	• Have you considered a connection between the seriousness of your circumstance and the level of impatience you feel toward God?
	• What does impatience look like?
	• How does impatience show up organizationally?
	• Are you able to read when employees are impatient with you?
	• What emotions show up for you when you are impatient?
	• How do you hold your impatience in check?
	• Who can you express impatience to?
	• Are there methods in place to gauge the effect impatience is having on you?
Principle #12: Patience (Round #2)	• Are you in a season of waiting?
	• Is a tenacious prayer life embedded in this period of waiting?
	• Have you considered the possibility that God is waiting because He wants to exalt you at the proper time?
	• Are you at peace in these periods of waiting?

Principle #13: The Motorboat and the Sailboat	• Under which conditions are you most likely to rely on your own power and intellect? • Do you have a pride meter? • How does pride show up for you? • Are there people on your leadership team that can hold you accountable from a pride point of view? • How do you confront pride in the workplace? • How do you acknowledge success and progress? • Where does pride show up in your organization?
Principle #14: The Companionway	• When do you like being around people? • When do you need a break from people? • Do those that work with you know the answers to the first two questions? • What are your desired methods of communication? • Where do you land on a scale of introversion and extroversion? • How does this impact relationships?
Principle #15: Waiting on God	• Do you believe Jeremiah 29:11? • Are there circumstances that you are contemplating right now? • Do you live with a peace that God will do exactly what he said he will do? • How does God speak to you?

Principle #16: The Fragility of Sailboats	• When do you feel vulnerable? • Are there emotions you can identify that have the potential of capsizing your ship? • Are there situations or circumstances that breed insecurities? • Have you ever discussed the idea of being fragile and what that does to your ability to lead?
Principle#17: Below the Waterline	• How are you doing below the waterline? (Give yourself a grade.) • Are there things that you need to confess to someone? • Have you ever considered the effect that these things might be having on your organization or leadership? • How do you keep your soul guarded against the enemy? • Is there a system of accountability embedded in your organization to guard the heart and keep it pure?
Principle #18: The Rudder and the Tongue	• What mistakes have been made in your leadership or organization related to this idea of the rudder and tongue? • Are your words or tone ever too much for the people you lead? • In what situations do you find it challenging to hold your tongue? • How might words be crafted to send a clearer message to the people you lead?

Principle #19: All Lines Are Organized	• When you consider the symbolism of all lines are organized, what thoughts are spurred regarding anything in your organization? • What are the major systems in your organization? • Are the systems in your organization efficient?
Principle #20: All Hands on Deck	• Are your expectations for all employees clear? • Are there people who do less than what is expected? • How is an excellent work ethic rewarded? • How do you handle employees who do not carry their weight? • Have you identified who the leaders in your organization are?
Principle #21: Man Overboard	• Do you have employees who are underperforming? • Are other employees frustrated with any team member for performance reasons? • When you hear the word "rogue," does any team member come to mind? • Is everyone clear on their responsibilities? • Are you comfortable and confident moving into a conversation regarding performance?
Principle #22: A Time to Be Captain	• Have you ever been widely criticized for being indecisive? • Have you ever been widely criticized for being too decisive? • Is the criticism fair? • Under what circumstances do you migrate to a style that is more autocratic?

References

The Holy Bible, HCSB.

The Holy Bible, NLT.

The Holy Bible, NIV.

The Holy Bible, KJV.

The Leadership Bible, 1998.

How to Listen to God, by Charles Stanley, 1985.

Courageous Conversations About Race, by Glenn E. Singleton and Curtis Linton, 2006.

The Will to Lead, The Skill to Teach: Transforming Schools at Every Level, by Anthony Muhammad and Sharroky Hollie, 2012.

Habits of Highly Effective People, by Stephen R. Covey, 1989.

The Thin Book of Trust, by Charles Feltman, 2009.

Printed in the United States
by Baker & Taylor Publisher Services